Experiencing God's Love

To Mrs Paulette Haye
From: Paulette James

Experiencing God's Love

Pacific Press® Publishing Association
Nampa, Idaho
Oshawa, Ontario, Canada
www.pacificpress.com

Designed by Steve Lanto

Additional copies of this book are available by calling toll-free 1-800-765-6955 or by visiting http://www.AdventistBookCenter.com.

ISBN 13: 978-0-8163-3404-9
ISBN 10: 0-8163-3404-8

12 13 14 15 16 • 5 4 3 2 1

Contents

Preface

Experiencing God's Love

The experience of a lifetime. It's a maxim so familiar that it's nearly lost its zing. Everywhere you turn someone beckons with an astonishing promise. Bungee jumping? The experience of a lifetime. Swimming with dolphins? The experience of a lifetime. Attractions of every stripe are pitched as the experience to beat all experiences. Each of them unique, exciting, and exhilarating.

But what if there was truly one experience that trumped all others? An encounter that not only bested every great moment in this life, but also promised to give you eternal bliss in the life to come? What would that experience look like?

That's the subject of this book. In the following pages, you'll discover a God who is so incredible, He will blow you away. You've never seen anything like Him. Not in your past. Not in your future. Not ever. And when His love washes over your soul, we think you'll agree—knowing Jesus Christ as your personal Savior is indeed the experience of a lifetime.

The men and women who write here know of what they speak. Their deep friendship with Jesus qualifies them to recommend Him without reservation. So read on, listen closely, and be amazed.

Pacific Press® Publishing Association

Chapter 1

Don't Worry—Be Happy!

Experiencing God's Grace

Dwight Nelson

In the bottom drawer of my desk is an old cassette tape (now you know how old it is!), with these words scribbled on its label "Don't Worry, Be Happy." Turns out it's a 1988 a cappella recording of composer-singer Bobby McFerrin, singing and whistling this jingle:

Here's a little song I wrote,
You might want to sing it note for note.
Don't worry, be happy.
In every life we have some trouble,
But when you worry you make it double.
Don't worry, be happy. . . .
'Cause when you worry, your face will frown,
and that will bring everybody down.
So don't worry, be happy!

But what's astounding is that this nursery rhyme bit of feel-good, quick-fix philosophy stole the ear of the nation that year, skyrocketing to the top of the charts, selling eighteen million copies and garnering two Grammy Awards! The entire world was playing the song, but Bobby McFerrin eventually resolved never to sing the song again after it had been given a political spin in an election campaign.[1]

But we do worry, don't we, no matter how catchy the tuneful admonition not to? After all, just look at our economy. We've all clucked our tongues at poor Greece with its awful indebtedness, all the while our own nation seems destined to go down that same sinkhole. And all this season's presidential campaign rhetoric notwithstanding, do you really think there's a human "savior" for our predicament?

"Don't worry, be happy!" But we do worry, and we're not happy. The February 2012 headline of the Medical News Today Web site would catch anybody's eye: "Suicide Rates Highest in 15 Years, US." The news release read,

> The National Suicide Prevention Lifeline, an emergency crisis hotline, revealed that the

> volume of calls they received between 2010 and 2011 increased by 14%.
>
> The increase in suicide rates has prompted the CDC [Center for Disease Control and Prevention] to recommend increasing job placement counseling, as well as financial services that can help to lower the mental distress that can increase the risk of [an] individual committing suicide.[2]

Let's face it. "Grin and bear it" and "don't worry, be happy" just don't cut it anymore, do they? We can sing the words until we're blue in the face, but deep down inside of our souls, you and I both know the specter of worry and anxiety is never that far away.

Consider these lines from the ancient writer Jeremiah—the one they still call the "weeping prophet." With his tissue box crammed with worries over what lies dead ahead for his beloved nation and hometown of Jerusalem, Jeremiah has for decades now been warning his neighbors of impending judgment and imminent disaster. The problem, quite frankly, is that when "don't worry, be happy" is your credo, there's only so much predicted "doom and gloom" you're willing to countenance. This is why, like a politician, the prophet's approval ratings have plummeted.

But then one day the headlines do the same, suddenly plunging into nonstop bad news. Overnight the economy is in shambles; unemployment skyrocketing; the inner city melting down into dark social decay; society is in an unstaunched moral hemorrhage. The news could hardly be worse. *Can it be that the cantankerous prophet has been right all along? Are we under divine judgment for the mess we've made of it all?* Nobody's whistling "Don't Worry, Be Happy" anymore. And as proof that the bad news can get "badder," the populace wakes up one morning to find their mortal enemy, Babylon, with thousands of armed hellions camping literally on Jerusalem's doorstep. The end is near!

But then—and here's what is so astonishing, especially to us who've been living with our own litany of incessant bad news headlines lately—in the midst of all that terrible news, the God of the universe interrupts their gloom and doom with one of the most breathtaking good news "don't worry, be happy" promises you've ever read! Straight from the heart of the Eternal to them and, given the similarity of the times, unbelievably good news straight from Him to you and me too.

Look what Jeremiah scribbled down:

> The LORD has appeared of old to me, saying:
> "Yes, I have loved you with an everlasting
> love;
> Therefore with lovingkindness I have drawn
> you.
> Again I will build you, and you shall be re-
> built,
> O virgin of Israel!
> You shall again be adorned with your tam-
> bourines,
> And shall go forth in the dances of those who
> rejoice" (Jeremiah 31:3, 4 NKJV).

Dancing with joy and tambourines? You've got to be kidding! "Don't worry, be happy" on the eve of imminent destruction? Are you crazy!

But that is precisely God's promise. Read it again:

> I have loved you with an everlasting love;
> therefore I have continued my faithfulness
> to you.

> Again I will build you, and you shall be built,
>   O virgin Israel!
> Again you shall take your tambourines,
>   and go forth in the dance of the
>   merrymakers (verses 3, 4, NRSV).

And why are the "merrymakers" dancing? The only explanation for such unbridled joy is the stunning news that this God of the universe loves us—can you believe this?—with an *everlasting* love! How does He put it? "I have loved you with an everlasting love; I have drawn you with unfailing kindness" (verse 3, NIV). Think about it. *Everlasting* has to mean just that—"lasting forever," which means that no matter how many times others have quit on us, there is Someone who won't.

Let's face it—Peter Gillquist is right:

> "We have become such a nation of self-lovers. Nothing is too sacred to leave—if we feel like it. We leave school if it gets boring or difficult; we leave home and parents if we're displeased; we leave our jobs, our marriages, and our churches."[3]

Is there a heart alive that doesn't know that

wrenching pain of someone we love leaving us? No wonder the merrymakers are dancing! For here is the promise that at last there is Someone who won't quit on us. No matter how many times we have failed ourselves, failed others, or failed Him, His love won't walk out on us.

Why even when we quit trusting God, He doesn't quit believing in us. For forty years the weeping prophet pleaded with his hometown to return to God. But for forty years nobody from the king on down gave God the time of day. And then all hell breaks loose and it looks like it's curtains. And what is the "overnighted" promise from God that Jeremiah hurriedly delivers to the doomed? "I have loved you with an *everlasting* love; I have drawn you with unfailing kindness." To a people who had wasted their lives and blown their chances comes this promise of God's *everlasting* love. Forever.

This is precisely what He was *dying* to tell us on the rocky summit of a hill called Golgotha. When Jesus stretched out His arms and they nailed Him to that bloody cross, it was the apex of the crimson truth about God's *everlasting* love. Why the very posture into which He was physically pinned, arms outstretched in a nailed-open embrace, His head and feet perpendicular to those arms, there Jesus was suspended on that gibbet between heaven and earth—a living, dying, quivering "plus sign" (+), revealing to the world an *everlasting* love, ever seeking to add (+) one more broken life to Himself.

Did you catch His dying prayer? "Father, forgive them, for they do not know what they do" (Luke 23:34, NKJV). *Everlasting* love, even in the face of death? The portrait of God never shone more brightly than in that death prayer, did it? For by praying that prayer, Jesus revealed the ultimate truth that any human can ever discover about God—that He is by nature a relentless Lover and an unconditional Forgiver. It is not only second nature to Him, it is His first nature too.

And that point is essential because some paint a harsh, stern picture of God, claiming that He needed the Cross to turn Him from an Accuser to a Forgiver. But the shining portrait of Calvary's death prayer is not of One who needed to climb the hill to *become* a Forgiver. He climbed it because He *was* and *is* a Forgiver.

God didn't need Calvary to change His mind about us. He needed Calvary to change our minds about Him.

"I have *always* loved you with an *everlasting* love," He says to us.

Relentless love! Unconditional forgiveness!

And did you notice that on that fateful Friday, the one we now call *Good* Friday, there was not a single soul atop that hill who asked to be forgiven, save for a dying thief at the end of the day? Not one of the jeering Roman warriors, not one of the cursing spectators, not one of the haughty clerics—nobody except for a small-time, backwoods robber asked for forgiveness. And yet from His bloody perch Jesus gazed down on that unrepentant mob and breathed His prayer: "Father, please! It doesn't matter. Forgive all of them. They don't know what they're doing." They murdered Him, the Innocent One—and yet His prayer *for them* was the quiet "Forgive them all." Apparently, *everlasting* really is true.

In his disturbing book *The Sunflower,* the late Simon Wiesenthal relives the gripping, dark narrative of that moment when he was secretly removed one day from his work detail as a young Jewish prisoner in a Nazi concentration camp and led by an expressionless nurse up the stairs and down the hallway of a nearby Polish hospital. At last he found himself (despite his nervous fear and better judgment) standing by the bedside of a dying Nazi SS soldier, his face entirely bandaged except for four openings—one for the mouth, one for the nose, and two for the ears. Yellow stains oozed through the bandages where the eyes must have been. The nurse left and the soldier groped for the hand of the boy. And when, with a hoarse whisper, the man spoke, what tumbled forth was the surreal but tortured confession of an act of genocide against a house filled with 150 to 200 helpless Jews. Haunted by the nightmares of his complicity in that awful crime, the dying man's last desperate request to his nurse had been for a Jew, any Jew, to whom he might confess his sin. And so, Will you forgive me? was the plea of the bandaged head. Wiesenthal describes the raging battle within his own young heart as he sat in the shadows beside that bed: Shall I forgive him or shall I not? At last, without a word, he left the room.

Twenty-five years later, still haunted by that deathbed confession and his decision not to forgive, Simon Wiesenthal—who miraculously survived the Holocaust but lost eighty-six family members and loved ones to it—ends his narrative with these words: "You, who have just read this sad and tragic episode in my life, can mentally change places with me and ask yourself the crucial question, 'What would I have done?' "[4]

What would I have done? What would you have done? We know what Jesus of Nazareth would have done—we just heard Him pray, "Father, forgive them, for they do not know what they do." It is the prayer of an *everlasting* love, is it not? And if He prayed that for His executioners, if He prayed that for the thieves between whom He was nailed, if He prayed that prayer for the rabble who throttled His cross, would He not pray that same prayer for the dying Nazi, would He not pray it for the living and dying likes of you and me, as well? In fact, is there a sin so heinous, is there a sinner so reprehensible that God's *everlasting* love could not forgive, did not forgive, that Friday outside of Jerusalem?

Consider these profound words from *The Desire of Ages,* the devotional classic on the life of Jesus:

> That prayer of Christ for His enemies ["Father, forgive them"] embraced the world. *It took in every sinner that had lived or should live, from the beginning of the world to the end*

> *of time.* Upon all rests the guilt of crucifying the Son of God. To all, forgiveness is freely offered. "Whosoever will" may have peace with God, and inherit eternal life.[5]

Did you catch that? You and I—all of us, the whole world, the entire human race—we were all forgiven that Friday long ago! "To all, forgiveness is freely offered." No matter how you have lived, no matter what you have done. There are only two words to describe a forgiveness that full and that free: *everlasting love.*

Do you realize what that means? When you fail and fall and your sin is splattered all over your heart and you are overwhelmed with your own guilt, when you've already confessed that sin a thousand times before, when your tortured conscience taunts you into giving up and quitting on God—don't. Instead, remember that God is by nature—He cannot be otherwise and be Himself—a relentless Lover and an unconditional Forgiver. In your guilt, throw yourself into Calvary's outstretched embrace. Not because God has to be persuaded but because I need to be reminded of the staggering price of *my* sin, the staggering cost of *His* love.

Everlasting love.

> I have loved you with an everlasting love;
> therefore I have continued my faithful-
> ness to you.
> Again I will build you, and you shall be built,
> O virgin Israel!
> Again you shall take your tambourines,
> and go forth in the dance of the merry-
> makers (Jeremiah 31:3, 4, NRSV).

Don't worry—when you come to Me—be happy!

When you hear God speaking those words, it is no wonder that the heart feels like dancing! For on an old summit, we have found a new song in God's heart.

It is the song of relentless love and outrageous grace.

A song you, too, can sing and share.

Forever.

Dwight Nelson is Senior Pastor of the Pioneer Memorial Seventh-day Adventist Church in Berrien Springs, Michigan.

---

1. You can listen to Bobby McFerrin singing and whistling his own lyrics, and you'll see why. See http://www.youtube.com/watch?v=_cVWrIQl7fU.

2. "Suicide Rates Highest in 15 Years, US," Medical News Today, February 20, 2012, accessed April 11, 2012, http://www.medicalnewstoday.com/articles/241911.php.

3. Peter E. Gillquist, *Why We Haven't Changed the World* (Old Tappan, N.J.: Revell, 1982), 56, 57, quoted in Ronald Sider, *The Scandal of the Evangelical Conscience* (Grand Rapids, Mich.: Baker Books), 90.

4. Simon Wiesenthal, *The Sunflower* (New York: Schocken Books), 98.

5. Ellen G. White, *The Desire of Ages* (Nampa, Idaho: Pacific Press® Publishing Association), 745; emphasis added.

Chapter 2

Be Anxious for Nothing

Experiencing God's Peace

Derek J. Morris

I met Sjarón on a recent trip to Namibia. She shared a testimony that I will never forget. Sjarón was a colicky baby. She cried almost constantly for the first three years of her life. Instead of seeking God's help and strength during this time, her exhausted mother put her in the care of a local family who submitted this innocent baby to black magic rituals. Her life became controlled by demons.

Sjarón grew up with the delusion that her only salvation would be found through immersing herself more and more deeply in the occult world. She discovered that many so-called Christians were powerless to resist her occult powers. On one occasion, when she entered a church, the pastor, who had been busy talking, suddenly found himself unable to speak anymore. He started coughing and stuttering until he grew red in the face. On another occasion, two professed Christians came to her apartment. When they entered the front door, everything went black. One fell over and could not get up. The other one pulled his friend out the front door while furniture moved around in the apartment. They notified their pastor, and he tried to reach out to Sjarón, but it was obvious to her that he was spiritually careless and unprotected. In fact, he laughed at her when she warned him he was contending with supernatural forces. Instead, he should have learned a lesson from the story of the sons of Sceva (Acts 19:13–16). It is dangerous and foolish to walk unprotected onto any battlefield, including a spiritual one. Within a couple of weeks, the pastor's ministry had collapsed.

In all of these encounters, Sjarón experienced power, but she was destitute of peace. "It was like holding a lot of lions on leashes in one hand and a whip in the other hand," she said as she attempted to describe her life. "You have to constantly feed and whip every single lion; otherwise, the one that you are not controlling will turn around and bite you. You never have rest or peace. You cannot even sleep." Such is the "good life" that Satan offers people apart from God. It is a delusion and a snare.

You ask, How did Sjarón find freedom from Satan's cruel power? How did she experience God's peace? Not as a result of the prayers of her parents. They were also deeply involved in the occult. Rather, God used some young Christian medical students at the university that she attended. She joined a study group with two of them. Unlike the other professed Christians that Sjarón had met, these young medical students were fully devoted to Jesus Christ as their Savior and Lord, and they were radically protected. Her demons could not reach them. Through those two Christian medical students, God led Sjarón to a personal relationship with Jesus as her Savior and Lord. They prayed *for* her and *with* her. Slowly but steadily, she came to the realization that the God of heaven was far more powerful than Satan. Finally, she surrendered her life to Jesus as her Savior and experienced the peace that only He can give. That is the unforgettable lesson that Sjarón taught me: only God can give you peace.

In the midst of this troubled world, God wants you to experience His peace. Do you need peace today? I'm not referring to the world's peace. That is merely a temporary cessation of hostility that can be reversed at any moment. God wants to give you His deep, abiding peace that no one can take from you. Are you interested?

God wants you to experience peace in your relationship with Him and peace in the midst of the challenges and trials of this life. How can we experience peace in our relationship with God? The apostle Paul gives us the answer in his inspired testimony to Christians in Rome: "Having been justified by faith, we have peace with God through our Lord Jesus Christ" (Romans 5:1).[1]

Jesus revealed the truth about our heavenly Father: God loves us. He is not out to catch us in our sin; He wants to save us from our sin. He doesn't want to damn us; He wants to deliver us. He is not against us; He is for us. Listen to the words of Jesus, recorded by the apostle John: "God so loved the world that He gave His only begotten Son, that whoever believes in Him should not perish but have everlasting life" (John 3:16). Our sin, guilt, and shame have separated us from God, but He wants to forgive all of our sins and "cleanse us from all unrighteousness" (1 John 1:9). He allowed His Son to be treated as we deserve and longs to treat us as Jesus deserves if we accept the gift of His grace. If we believe this precious truth, repeated numerous times in the Word of God, we will discover peace with God through our Lord Jesus Christ.

John grew up with this misconception that his good deeds somehow recommended him to God and that his sins caused God to be angry with him. Perhaps, if he were adequately well behaved, John thought, God might even like him. When he stumbled and fell, the adversary was right there to remind him that he was unacceptable to God. He just wasn't good enough.

The apostle Paul turns that idea upside down with the bold declaration that God loves us even when we are dead in our trespasses and sins. When we look our worst, He comes looking for us. He comes to seek and to save the lost (Luke 19:10). God loves us too much to violate our free will, but He will do everything within His power to save us. He loves us and wants to spend eternity with us. That is the amazing truth that Jesus came to proclaim.[2] When John finally caught a glimpse of God's amazing love, revealed in the Person of His Son, Jesus Christ, he accepted the precious gift of salvation and experienced peace with God.

God wants you to experience His peace—peace in your relationship with Him and also peace in the midst of the challenges of life. Listen to the words of Jesus: "Peace I leave with you, My peace I give to you; not as the world gives do I give to you. Let not your heart be troubled, neither let it be afraid" (John 14:27). "These things I have spoken to you, that in Me you may have peace. In the world you will have tribulation; but be of good cheer, I have overcome the world" (John 16:33).

What circumstances of life threaten to rob you of peace? Sickness? Economic hardship? Persecution? How is it possible to experience God's peace in the midst of the challenges of life? First, as followers of Jesus, as people of hope, we can remind ourselves that this time of suffering is only temporary. The apostle Paul faced many adversities. He shared this testimony with the Christians in Corinth: "We are hard pressed on every side, yet not crushed; we are perplexed, but not in despair; persecuted, but not forsaken; struck down, but not destroyed" (2 Corinthians 4:8, 9). How could Paul experience peace in the midst of these challenges? He answers our question in the same letter to believers in Corinth:

> We do not lose heart. Even though our outward man is perishing, yet the inward man is being renewed day by day. For our light affliction, which is but for a moment, is working for us a far more exceeding and eternal weight of glory, while we do not look at the things which are seen, but at things which are not seen. For the things which are seen are temporary, but the things which are not seen are eternal (verses 16–18).

Paul reminds us that the challenges of this life that threaten to rob us of our peace are only temporary. A better day is coming. "Weeping may endure for a night, but joy comes in the morning" (Psalm 30:5). Paul chose to fix his attention on things that are eternal. In his inspired letter to the Colossians, Paul wrote, "Set your mind on things above, not on things on the earth. For you died, and your life is hidden with Christ in God. When Christ who is our life appears, then you also will appear with Him in glory" (Colossians 3:2–4).

That is our blessed hope—the "glorious appearing of our great God and Savior Jesus Christ" (Titus 2:13). When Jesus returns in glory, you also will appear with Him in glory. That precious assurance puts the challenges of this life into a new perspective. We can experience God's peace in the midst of sickness, hardship, and persecution because we know that the challenges of this life are only temporary.

We can also have peace in the midst of life's challenges because Jesus has promised that He will never leave us or forsake us (Hebrews 13:5). We do not face these hardships alone. Jesus is with us. He gave this promise to His followers: " 'I am with you always, even to the end of the age.' Amen" (Matthew 28:20). And I also say, "Amen!" Jesus will never leave us or forsake us. He sends His Spirit to be with us and in us. He commissions holy angels to protect us. We do not need to live in fear. We can live serenely, filled with God's abiding peace, because He is with us.

During a recent visit to Australia, I met two sisters who had grown up as the children of missionaries in the Solomon Islands. They gave me a remarkable book—their family biography, titled *Broken Stick*.[3] Their family faced many hardships and trials, but they experienced peace in the midst of those trials because they knew that Jesus was with them. On one occasion, a local chief invited their father, Norman Ferris, to visit a village on the east coast of Guadalcanal, one of the Solomon Islands. Happy to respond to the request, Norman traveled with the chief to his village and taught the villagers Christian songs. He also hung a picture roll on a tree and told stories about Jesus.

I have no doubt that the angels in heaven rejoiced as they witnessed the scene. Men and women were receiving the truth about Jesus with joy, but Satan was angry. Having ruled that island for many years, he wasn't about to yield his territory without a fight. Satan came to Nghata, the devil priest of that region. "Nghata, today a White man came to Koilotumria," Satan announced. "He is dangerous! He will bring disharmony to our people. You must take your sword. Go soon and kill him." Satan's instructions were clear and in harmony with his evil character.

That evening the people of Koilotumria were gathered together, learning more songs about Jesus. No one noticed the devil priest as he slipped unnoticed into their village under the cover of darkness. But as the villagers sang "Jesus Loves Me," Nghata's heart became filled with hate and fury. Grasping his sword, he rushed toward the missionary with a mighty yell.

When Norman Ferris realized what was happening, he didn't run in fear. Rather, his heart was filled with peace as he prayed this simple prayer: "Dear God, send Your mighty arm of power." The Lord instantly and powerfully responded to his prayer, supernaturally stopping Nghata dead in his tracks. Unable to move, the man could not carry out his murderous plan. Quickly, the local villagers overpowered the devil priest. God had spared Norman Ferris's life.[4]

Ferris claimed the promise given more than twenty-seven hundred years earlier through the prophet Isaiah:

> "You will keep him in perfect peace,
> Whose mind is stayed on You,
> Because he trusts in You.
> Trust in the LORD forever,
> For in YAH, the LORD, is everlasting strength"
> (Isaiah 26:3, 4).

But Norman wasn't the only person who experienced God's peace there in the Solomon Islands. Not long after that remarkable deliverance, Nghata, the devil priest, also realized that he needed the peace that only God can give. Like my friend

Sjarón, Nghata realized that Satan could not give him peace. Only God can give you peace. Nghata trusted Jesus as his personal Savior and Lord, was baptized, and became a mighty worker for God. The Lord used that former devil priest to establish two Christian churches in his region. Today, sixteen churches with more than two thousand members thrive on an island once ruled by Satan. The chains of the enemy are being broken. People are finding freedom and experiencing God's peace, even in the midst of the challenges of this life.

You may not face a crisis as severe as an assassination attempt by a devil priest, but you will certainly face many challenges that could rob you of your peace. Whatever the challenge, you can experience God's peace as you remember that Jesus is right there by your side.

Our son Jonathan taught me an important lesson about experiencing God's peace. During the time that our two little boys were growing up, my wife, Bodil, had an idea, one that she refers to as an inspiration from God. She noticed that she could still remember all the nursery rhymes she had learned as a child—rhymes such as "Mary Had a Little Lamb" and "Humpty Dumpty Sat on a Wall." So she thought, *What if I chose sayings from the Word of God, put them to music, and then helped our children memorize them? Will those words be safely stored in their hearts to be then remembered by them in times of need?* Our experience as a family has answered that question with a resounding Yes.

One of the Scripture songs that Bodil composed was taken from the apostle Paul's inspired letter to Christians in Philippi:

> Be anxious for nothing, but in everything by prayer and supplication, with thanksgiving, let your requests be made known to God; and the peace of God, which surpasses all understanding, will guard your hearts and minds through Christ Jesus (Philippians 4:6, 7).

We sang that song together in family worship and hid the precious Word of God in our hearts.

When our youngest son, Jonathan, was about ten years old, he developed an interest in mountain biking and became the happy owner of a white Trek 830 mountain bike. He wanted his daddy to ride along with him, so I purchased a bright-green Trek 8000 mountain bike with a front shock absorber—I wasn't as agile as my ten-year-old son. Do you know what we discovered when we started mountain biking together? The world is full of dogs! It seems that they like to chase bicycles, especially *my* bicycle. I had some negative encounters with dogs when I was younger; so when a dog chases me, I assume it intends to bite me.

One day, Jonathan and I decided to ride our bikes near our home. I took the lead, and my son followed close behind me. We were both wearing our helmets, and we were ready for a pleasant ride—or so I thought. About a mile from our house, we were happily pedaling along the side of the road when in my peripheral vision I saw a big, dark mass hurtling in my direction. Glancing around, I saw it was a large black dog. It looked like a mixture between a rottweiler and a pit bull, and it was racing straight toward my bike. Panicking, I began to pedal at a furious rate. Soon I began hyperventilating, and my heart was pounding. To my dismay, the dog was gaining ground. With one last burst of energy, I surged forward. In a few seconds, I was safe!

For a moment, a feeling of euphoria settled over me, but then I remembered something vital—

I am a parent! Jonathan had been riding right behind me—at least he had been the last time I had checked. Pulling off the road, I stopped and turned around, hoping not to witness a bloody tragedy. My son was calmly pedaling his bike, the big black dog just sitting by the side of the road, watching him go by. The animal didn't even bark at him!

When Jonathan caught up with me, I said, "Did you see that huge black dog?"

"Yes, Daddy. When I saw the dog, the first thought that came into my mind was to sing 'The angel of the Lord encampeth round about them that fear him, and delivereth them' [Psalm 34:7, KJV]. Then I sang, 'Be anxious for nothing, but in everything by prayer and supplication, with thanksgiving, let your requests be made known to God; and the peace of God, which surpasses all understanding, will guard your hearts and minds through Christ Jesus' " (Philippians 4:6, 7).

The promises of God are true, my friends. You can experience God's peace, a peace that surpasses all understanding. God wants you to experience His peace today—peace with Him through faith in Jesus as your Lord and Savior, and peace in the midst of the challenges of this life—knowing that

He will never leave you nor forsake you. Do you want to experience God's peace today? Then reach out to Him in faith. And then rejoice today that in a world filled with anxiety, where people's hearts are failing them for fear (Luke 21:26), God wants you to experience His peace.

Derek J. Morris is Editor of Ministry *magazine.*

---

1. Unless otherwise noted, the Bible quotations in this chapter are from the New King James Version.

2. Read Luke 15.

3. Eileen E. Lantry, *Broken Stick: Mission to the Forbidden Islands* (Hagerstown, Md.: Review and Herald® Publishing Association, 2010).

4. Ibid., 37, 38.

Chapter 3

His Loss Is Your Gain

Experiencing God's Presence

Jonathan Henderson

Maybe it was an act of desperation. No, probably more an act of passion. Certainly, nothing less than an act of total submission. It was violent. It was bloody. And there was lots of screaming, crying, and tears. The pain was the most intense known to human beings. Entombed in darkness with days of no consciousness. No, this is not the story of Mount Calvary. This is the story of another hill. Three days in the belly of the earth? Try nine months in the belly of Mary. Jesus' first few moments on earth were every bit as graphic and violent as His last. Paul described this as the process of becoming nothing:

> Who, being in very nature God,
> did not consider equality with God some-

> thing to be used to his own advantage;
> rather, he made himself nothing
> by taking the very nature of a servant,
> being made in human likeness (Philippians 2:6, 7, NIV).

Nothingness. God, who transcends everything, now descends below everything. Supposedly, the universe can't contain Him, but now a uterus can? God, who is spirit, becomes flesh. The Creator seemingly becomes the created (John 1:3, 14; John 4:24). Paul calls this a mystery. The "mystery of godliness" (1 Timothy 3:16, KJV). Emmanuel—God with us.

So maybe this is not the way you imagined the "silent night" of Jesus' birth. It's definitely not how I imagined it until recently. You see, my wife and I are expecting. It's our first. This is supposed to be a beautiful and celebrated period in our lives. Honestly, it's not. There's vomiting; frequent trips to the bathroom interrupting the night; and hormonal level fluctuations that are downright scary. Her immune system is compromised. She has back pain, sore feet, migraine headaches, and unpredictable cravings. And that's only a precursor to what I believe must be the worst part: labor. And we pray it's not the twenty-three-hour variety. Then there is tearing, screaming, more blood, and other stuff I'm wishing I didn't see in the videos that are supposed to prepare me but only scare me more. Why don't people talk about this side of pregnancy and birth? Though I'm certain that childbirth was a pleasant experience before sin entered this world, it now makes me wish that a stork would drop the baby off on our front doorstep. And though God could have chosen a million other ways to send His Son to us, this was His vehicle of choice. Theologians call it the Incarnation. I call it *Ahhhhhhhh!*

Now, some would think I'm focusing on all the negative aspects of having a child. "Once you see your baby's face, it will all be worth it," I can hear the gallery saying. And I keep asking myself, *What makes looking at my image worth all the pain and suffering? Is seeing my eyes on her or my nose on him really worth the Herculean effort?* And for God, what makes it worth it? His life on earth is bookended with darkness, blood, and a loss of consciousness. What could possibly drive the Creator to the conclusion that this must be the only way to rescue us from the fatal disease of sin?

My favorite movie while growing up was about my favorite superhero—Superman. He's my favorite because he was the most powerful. Superstrength, power of flight, heat vision, X-ray vision, superbreath—you get the point. And what made *Superman 2* the best movie was that he squared off against three villains from his home planet of Krypton with the exact same superpowers. This was the perfect setup for any eight-year-old looking for presumably insurmountable odds against his hero. However, nothing could have ever prepared me for the real enemy, more formidable than the villainous three—Lois Lane! That's right. The hard-nosed, sassy reporter, with no superpowers, I might add, single-handedly takes out the Man of Steel. Superman falls in love with Lois so intensely that he's willing to give up all his powers so he can become normal, average—human. Superman gets into a Kryptonian machine that irreversibly reduces his powers to that of a human so he can appear to fit more easily into Lois's life. No longer super—just a man. Not a man of steel. Now, a man of flesh.

Love compels a person to do things that otherwise would be unthinkable. Love moves a person to take risks that in any other situation would be unimaginable.

So what drives God to make this trek into a world of irreversible change? I believe that in order to discover the answer to why God would want to become one of us, we must understand why He made us in the first place.

God is a risk taker. And no, that is not a sacrilegious statement. He is, and we're all risk takers too. We take risks every time we get behind the wheel of a car. It's risky every time we eat at our favorite restaurant. That new promotion? Risky. Dating? Marriage? Having children? Risk, risk, and double risk. Couples have babies all the time, fully knowing the risks, such as sudden infant death syndrome (SIDS), mental and physical disabilities, and the possibility of their children developing future addictions. There is also the present-day reality that parents might have to financially support their children well into their thirties. An even a more painful possibility is that their children will grow up into adults with the capacity to completely reject and neglect them if they so choose. And with all those risks, we still want to have the little rascals!

There is risk in getting married. Although there is immense joy in finding the person who will love you unconditionally, you run the equal risk of that special someone eventually hating every fiber of your existence. So what do you do? Marry something not like you? You can marry a tree—tall, sturdy, dependable. No risk there. Neither is there much of a chance for any meaningful conversation or opportunity to be authentically loved in return. You can marry the squirrel in the tree. She wouldn't require you to spend a lot of money on her. A few acorns would satisfy her, and you could count on her to be faithful until the end. But then again, you are still missing the component of emotional and cognitive reflection. Sure, the squirrel gives you a few laughs because she's cute, but not because she has a great sense of humor. You can marry someone like you, "bone of [your] bones and flesh of [your] flesh" (Genesis 2:23, NIV). It will be risky, but it just might be worth it.

God created intelligent human beings in His *likeness*. Great were the risks and potential for us to choose something contrary to the blueprints of life because He endowed us with the freedom of choice. God was attracted to the idea of being in a consensual, loving relationship with humanity. He could have sheltered us from the choice of evil and pretended it didn't exist, but that would not have shown integrity and transparency. Adam and Eve deserved, at the very least, a choice. So God trusted them in the Garden of Paradise. Knowing fully well that they could crash the family car, He trusted them with the keys to the vehicle. He trusted them with the tree of knowledge of good and evil in the heavily trafficked intersection of the Garden. God did not hide it in a corner and cover it with cobwebs. He could have placed an electric fence around the tree, but that would not have shown trust in His new creation. God placed it right next to the remote for the television. No parental lock or password required. They could watch any TV show or commercial peddling the product and propaganda of the serpent in the tree, who we now know as God's number one adversary, Satan. They could hear the enemy's campaign speech at any time.

God could not entertain a relationship with His new companions that was not based on free will. Love can be genuine only in freedom, even if that same freedom meant that God could end up losing us.

Unfortunately, the couple chose a different path. They wrecked the car. They cast their vote for another administration. And as a result, sin entered the world. On the day that Adam and Eve sinned, God came to visit them in the Garden. On this occasion, they were nowhere to be found. "Where are you? Why are you hiding?" God asked Adam and Eve (see Genesis 3:9). Interestingly enough, He has been asking that question of us ever since. Our sinfulness makes God look scary and angry. We run from Him instead of to Him. The sound of God's footsteps used to bring such a thrill of anticipation, but the knowledge and familiarity with evil had distorted that sound and made it dreadful. Sin has now made God appear and sound like Godzilla. So what is He to do? He wants to talk to us, but we think He's shouting. He wants to hear us out, but we think He's deaf to our cries. He wants to see us, but we prefer to hide. He wants us to see Him, but would we even dare look? Why was it necessary for Jesus to come to earth? Because we kept running and hiding. Because a God in diapers, or learning how to walk, isn't scary at all. So, He became one of us. It was the only way He could draw us out of hiding.

God beckoned to us from the shadows through His friendship with Abraham, but was unsuccessful. He attempted to draw us out through His faithfulness to Joseph, but that was also ineffective. He even tried with His laws, given through Moses, but that just made Him look arbitrary. From King David, who had a heart like God's, to Daniel, whose prophecies and prayers convinced a nation to hope again, men and women continued to run and hide from their Creator. God's friends were never perfect "reps." So if you need a job well done, then you better do it yourself, right? So in fulfillment of the promise God made to Adam and Eve, He came to us personally. He would show us His love, kindness, compassion, and patience in such a real, practical, and intimate way that there would be no mistaking what He is like. God would no longer be scary. God would be approachable. Children would want to play around Him. God would finally draw us out of hiding. The author of the book of Hebrews writes the following:

> In the past God spoke to our ancestors through the prophets many times and in many different ways. But now in these last

> days God has spoken to us through his Son. God has chosen his Son to own all things, and through him he made the world. The Son reflects the glory of God and shows exactly what God is like (Hebrews 1:1–3, NCV).

Jesus knew of the importance of knowing and experiencing God for who He truly is that He equated it to eternal life. "This is eternal life: that they may *know you,* the only true God, and Jesus Christ, whom you have sent" (John 17:3, NIV; emphasis added). God came in order to be known. He knew that you would choose Him and His will if you only knew the truth. If you only knew Him, He would get your vote.

So maybe the night wasn't so silent, but the message was loud and clear. God became one with us. Why? Look no further than the image you see in the mirror. Hebrews tells us that for the joy of *us,* He came and endured (Hebrews 12:2). In a world that tells us we should make something of ourselves, God made Himself nothing. When the angels sang, "Glory to God in the highest" on the night of His birth, Jesus was below, in a manger. It was a place of total vulnerability and risk—a place where God loses His muscles and superpowers. Christ became nothing so that we could become something. He took one look at you, His love and His joy, smiled, and said, "It was all worth it."

Jonathan Henderson is Lead Pastor of the Grand Advent Seventh-day Adventist Church in Oakland, California.

Chapter 4

Scandalous Grace

Experiencing God's Forgiveness

Karl Haffner

"I know in my head that God has forgiven me," the student sobbed, "but in my gut I know better—God will *never* forgive me for the abortion."

Tentatively, I asked, "Do you think your mistake is any more offensive to God than—"

"It wasn't just a 'mistake,' " she snarled. "It was murder. And, yes, I think God has a harder time forgiving murder than He does for cheating on a quiz or something."

By the end of our conversation, I sensed this young woman was only more entrenched in the notion that God would never forgive her for what she deemed was the unpardonable sin. I tried to convince her otherwise. I escorted her through a ton of texts that sing of God's forgiveness.

- "In him we have redemption through his blood, the forgiveness of sins, in accordance with the riches of God's grace" (Ephesians 1:7).[1]
- "The Lord our God is merciful and forgiving, even though we have rebelled against him" (Daniel 9:9).
- "He has rescued us from the dominion of darkness and brought us into the kingdom of the Son he loves, in whom we have redemption, the forgiveness of sins" (Colossians 1:13, 14).
- "As far as the east is from the west, so far has he removed our transgressions from us" (Psalm 103:12).
- "There is now no condemnation for those who are in Christ Jesus" (Romans 8:1).

The young woman believed in the Bible. As she left my office, she quipped that our Bible study was "comforting." But she just couldn't transmute the texts into her story. She struggled to *experience* God's forgiveness.

Secretly, I've harbored some of her doubts. I believe in God's forgiveness. I preach about God's forgiveness. I understand what the Bible teaches about God's forgiveness. But when it comes to experiencing it, I fear that perhaps my account is overdrawn and that it threatens to bust God's Bank of Mercy. I have my questions.

Question 1: Does God forgive the big sin?

King David is the poster boy of the *big* sin. Oh, he committed a smorgasbord of sins to be sure, but the defining dent in his legacy would have to be his affair with Bathsheba and the subsequent murder of her husband, Uriah. Listen to David's tormented soul:

Your arrows have pierced me,
  and your hand has come down on me.
Because of your wrath there is no health in
    my body;
  there is no soundness in my bones because
    of my sin.
My guilt has overwhelmed me
  like a burden too heavy to bear.
My wounds fester and are loathsome
  because of my sinful folly.
I am bowed down and brought very low;
  all day long I go about mourning.
My back is filled with searing pain;

there is no health in my body.
I am feeble and utterly crushed;
I groan in anguish of heart (Psalm 38:2–8).

That's a cheery little passage, huh?

David's anguish reminds us of the distress that results when we fail to allow God to forgive that big, unforgivable mistake. Sin can eat you from the inside out. Ulcers, migraines, high blood pressure, and a host of other ailments are fertilized by unresolved sin. Psychiatrist Karl Menninger once claimed that if he could convince the patients in psychiatric hospitals that their sins were forgiven, 75 percent of them could walk out the next day. Clearly, experiencing God's forgiveness has enormous implications for one's spiritual, emotional, and physical health.

Failure to receive God's forgiveness for that big mistake imprisons the soul. Ask Hilda Verduzco. She's a mother of three from Dallas, Texas, who sits in jail. It started with a twenty-four-ounce strawberry alcoholic beverage at her boyfriend's house. She guzzled a bit more of the drink. Then she drove to pick up a friend for a night of partying.[2]

She never made it to the party. Nor does she remember the accident in which she broadsided Kina Williams's car. Both Kina and her two-year-old daughter Karmen were killed.

Now Verduzco grovels from a cell—begging for forgiveness. "I want to tell the family I'm so sorry. I know this doesn't cut it, but I am."[3] Verduzco asked her family to forgo her bail money and donate it instead to the Williams family for funeral expenses and other costs.

The family of the victims did not respond to Verduzco's apology. Whether or not she will ever feel forgiven remains unclear. "I deserve to be here," she says from behind bars. "I mean I deserve to rot in here. I deserve for them to throw away the key. I took two lives. What can I say?"[4]

Verduzco is right. She is exactly where she deserves to be.

But forgiveness travels into the tricky terrain of the undeserved. That's why forgiveness is so complex—it's never earned. It ventures from the domain of justice into the realm of grace. Informed by John Calvin, James C. Goodloe IV observes, "If we deserved forgiveness, we would not need it; and if forgiveness were based on our deserving it, we would forever despair of it, and our consciences would remain in perpetual terror."[5]

Perpetual terror—this is the state of the soul that cannot accept God's forgiveness. Now you can live in that state if you insist, but you do not need to. No matter how colossal your sin, it does not eclipse the margin of God's mercy.

Like David, you can find healing. He writes,

> Then I acknowledged my sin to you
> and did not cover up my iniquity.
> I said, "I will confess
> my transgressions to the LORD."
> And you forgave
> the guilt of my sin (Psalm 32:5).

Question 2: Does God forgive the same old sin, over and over and over and . . . ?

Maybe you skimmed over the *big* sin question; after all, you don't have an affair or a murder polluting your portfolio of failures. Yours is not the *big* public transgression but the little, compulsive private sins. Gossip, pornography, pride, gluttony—nothing that gets the attention of the church's disciplinary committee—but sins that derail you all the same. You wonder, *Does God get tired of hearing me confess this same old sin? At what point will He stop forgiving me?*

Perhaps you can relate to the character in Garrison Keillor's adventures from Lake Wobegon:

> Larry the Sad Boy . . . was saved twelve times in the Lutheran church, an all-time record. Between 1953 and 1961 he threw himself weeping and contrite on God's throne of grace on twelve separate occasions—and this in a Lutheran church that wasn't evangelical, had no altar call, no organist playing "Just As I Am Without One Plea" while a choir hummed and a guy with shiny hair took hold of your heartstrings and played you like a cheap guitar—this is the Lutheran church, not a bunch of hillbillies—these are Scandinavians, and they repent in the same way that they sin: discreetly, tastefully, at the proper time, and bring a Jell-O salad for afterward. . . . *Twelve times.* Even we fundamentalists got tired of him. . . . God didn't mean us to feel guilt all our lives. There comes a point when you should dry your tears and join the building committee and start grappling with the problems of the

> church furnace and . . . be of use, but Larry kept on repenting and repenting.[6]

Got a little Larry in ya? Tired of tramping back to the same old altar, repenting of the same old sin? If repentance really worked, at some point shouldn't your frequent flights to the confessional booth get canceled?

Take heart, my friend. Consider the words of a fellow struggler who wrestled with the same question.

> Just as through the disobedience of the one man the many were made sinners, so also through the obedience of the one man the many will be made righteous. The law was brought in so that the trespass might increase. But where sin increased, grace increased all the more, so that, just as sin reigned in death, so also grace might reign through righteousness to bring eternal life through Jesus Christ our Lord (Romans 5:19–21).

The apostle Paul makes it clear that through the sin of one man, namely Adam, we have all sinned. Even so, through the obedience of one Man, namely Jesus Christ, there is forgiveness. Yes, even forgiveness for that same old sin that keeps creeping back. Paul states that where that same old sin increased, grace increased even more. Simply put, there is forgiveness for that same old sin.

To steal a metaphor from the world of golf, you might think of it as a mulligan. A mulligan is when you shank a shot out-of-bounds or dribble it off the tee and you take a do-over. You don't count the shot. You don't write it down. It won't appear on the scorecard. It will be as if it never happened. There is no record of it. No questions asked. No penalties assigned. You get to do it over.

Wouldn't it be nice if this practice of taking mulligans could bleed into every arena of life? You're cruising in the triple digits down Interstate 5 when you get pulled over by a policeman. When he approaches your car, however, his face softens and he tenderly says, "Take a mulligan!" Or you haven't paid taxes in twenty years. Finally, the IRS catches up with you. The auditor informs you of a million-dollar debt in back taxes and penalties. Just as you pull out your checkbook to cover the bill, the IRS agent smiles and says, "Take a mulligan!" Maybe you stay up late watching Dave Letterman, Jay Leno, and six infomercials for the same ab machine. Your plan is to arise early to cram for a final exam. Instead, you sleep through your alarm and botch the test in spectacular style. Later that day your professor visits you with a new test that he has taken for you. You just need to sign your name. He hands you the fresh slate and says, "Take a mulligan!"

Can you imagine a world that's bursting with mulligans? It's hard to picture, isn't it? Our intuitive sense of justice defies the very notion of grace. That's why we struggle so with the question of whether or not God will keep forgiving us for the same sin. To give one mulligan is one thing. But to dole out a dozen mulligans on every hole, for the same exact shank, why that's ridiculous. That's scandalous. That's unfair.

That's grace.

Where sin abounds, grace abounds much more. Even though you may have fallen into the same pit numerous times before, there is grace for the repentant sinner. There is forgiveness every time—even for Larry, the Lake Wobegon professional repenter.

Question 3: Does God really forgive my sins?

While Scripture leaves little doubt about the all-encompassing and unending nature of God's forgiveness for *all* sin—no matter how big or how often—many of us still struggle to make it personal. It's one thing for King David or for the apostle Paul to experience God's forgiveness, but is it really possible for me?

Jesus emphatically answers from the cross.

> When you were dead in your sins and in the uncircumcision of your flesh, God made you alive with Christ. He forgave us all our sins, having canceled the charge of our legal indebtedness, which stood against us and condemned us; he has taken it away, nailing it to the cross. And having disarmed the powers and authorities, he made a public spectacle of them, triumphing over them by the cross (Colossians 2:13–15).

In your mind, make a list of your sins. Now nail that list to the Cross. Next, rejoice as the blood of Jesus washes over your list—be it the one big sin or a billion little ones—your sins are forgiven.

Your sins. Really. The grace of God washes over all your wrongdoing and you stand forgiven and free! You do not need to live in the prison of your sordid past any longer.

The March 11, 2011, issue of the *New York Times* featured the story of Robert Salzman, a fifty-one-year-old ex-convict who had spent nearly all of his adult life in prison. When he was released in 2001, Salzman struggled to adjust to his freedom outside of prison walls. He couldn't land steady employment or pay the bills. Instead, he bounced around homeless shelters, barely surviving.

His big break came in June 2010. While Salzman was riding a subway car in Manhattan, he was discovered by Rashaad Ernesto Green, a writer and director who was on the lookout for someone to play a grizzled former convict in his upcoming film. Green auditioned Salzman and awarded him a key role for the film.

In the following months, Salzman found it difficult to believe that he was actually free from prison. One time, while filming with Green on location in a Long Island penitentiary, an exhausted Salzman drifted to sleep on a mat in the cell. When he woke up, he was confused and believed he was still a prisoner. Salzman started weeping in despair—until it slowly occurred to him that he was, in fact, a free man. He could walk out of that dank dungeon any time he wished.[7]

No matter your past, you can find freedom from sin and condemnation. Just walk to the Cross. In Christ, you are free to experience forgiveness and freedom.

So will you cash in on Christ's offer?

A final question

Giving gift cards is the hot new trend for holidays and birthdays. Cards offer the recipient the choice to purchase whatever he or she wants from a particular store.

The downside to gift cards is that sometimes they carry expiration dates. More than once I've misplaced a card, only to find it after its value was deleted—compliments of that annoying "expiration date." One day a gift card can be worth one hundred dollars, and then the next day it has the value of a stack of Enron stock. You missed the opportunity to spend it!

Mike Silva points out that God's gift of forgiveness is like a gift card. It is more valuable than anything in the world. He purchased it with His Son's life, and He offers it to you. He begs of you to take it. If you fail to use it, however, then it holds no value. The price He paid at Calvary was in vain.[8]

A gift card is a useless slab of plastic unless it is redeemed. Similarly, God's forgiveness is empty prattle unless it is redeemed. Don't wait until it's too late.

Will you accept His gift?

Karl Haffner is Senior Pastor of the Kettering Seventh-day Adventist Church in Kettering, Ohio.

---

1. All Bible quotations in this chapter are from the New International Version.

2. Melissa Cutler, "Alleged Drunk Driver Begs Family for Forgiveness," KDFW News, November 22, 2010, accessed February 23, 2012, http://www.myfoxdfw.com/dpp/news/112210-drunk-driver-begs-family-for-forgiveness.

3. "Drunk Driving Suspect Has Message for Family," CBS DFW, November 22, 2010, accessed February 23, 2012, http://dfw.cbslocal.com/2010/11/22/drunk-driving-suspect-has-message-for-family/.

4. Melissa Cutler, "Alleged Drunk Driver Begs Family for Forgiveness."

5. James C. Goodloe IV, *Preaching Through Romans* (Richmond, Va.: n.p., 2004), PDF e-book, 48, accessed February 23, 2012, http://www.foundationrt.org/sermons/Romans/Preaching_through_Romans.pdf.

6. Garrison Keillor, "Exiles," in *Leaving Home* (New York: Penguin Books, 1990), 189, 190.

7. Corey Kilgannon, "Sidewalk Is His Prison Yard," *New York Times,* March 11, 2011, accessed April 12, 2012, http://www.nytimes.com/2011/03/13/nyregion/13sweat.html.

8. Mike Silva, *Would You Like Fries With That?* (Nashville, Tenn.: Thomas Nelson, 2005), 14.

Chapter 5

The Rest of Your Life

Experiencing God's Rest

Randy Roberts

I've got bad news, and I've got worse news, so we might as well start with the bad news: *I'm tired—and I'm not alone. A lot of us are tired.* In fact, if you say you're *not* tired, you may be out of step with a lot of other people. The frantic and frenetic pace of modern-day life leaves many of us exhausted. More than a few can relate to the person whom the group Alabama sang about in their hit song:

> I'm in a hurry to get things done
> Oh I rush and rush until life's no fun
> All I really gotta do is live and die
> But I'm in a hurry and don't know why.

That's the bad news. Now let me give you the worse news: *the weariness of our lives is not just physical, it's spiritual.* Can you relate to the words of the ancient prophet? " 'There is no peace,' says my God, 'for the wicked' " (Isaiah 57:21, NIV). Maybe Augustine was thinking of Isaiah when he wrote that the soul is restless until it finds its rest in God.

So the news isn't good at all; except for this—Jesus speaks to our situation. He knows of our weariness, our stress, our spiritual dis*ease*. And to all who experience such, He issues an invitation containing very good news.

"Come to me," He says, "all you who are weary and burdened, and I will give you rest. Take my yoke upon you and learn from me, for I am gentle and humble in heart, and you will find rest for your souls. For my yoke is easy and my burden is light" (Matthew 11:28–30, TNIV).

Jesus spoke these words in the context of people who were tired because they were struggling under the burden of endless rules. In fact, earlier in this same chapter of Matthew, He said some fairly harsh things to people who were really into church. Korazin and Bethsaida and Capernaum, all Jewish cities, were the recipients of very direct statements of woe pronounced upon them by Christ. Why? Because while these cities saw His deeds, they wouldn't repent of theirs.

The people who followed and listened to Jesus were up to their necks in goodness. Their lives overflowed with acts of devotion. The law of Moses was applied in every area of life. In fact, there were so many laws and duties that one commentator says a whole lifetime was not sufficient to learn them all.

As an example, consider these words: "The religion of the day was a 'religion . . . of burdens.' "

Even the rabbis saw this. A familiar, yet remorseful parable shows just how binding, constricting, burdensome, and impossible the demands of the law could be.

> "There was a poor widow . . . who had two daughters and a field. When she began to plough, Moses [i.e., the Law of Moses] said: 'You must not plough with an ox and [a donkey] together.' When she began to sow, he said: 'You must not sow your field with mingled seed.' When she began to reap and to make stacks of corn, he said: 'When you reap your harvest in your field, and have forgotten a sheaf in the field, you shall not go

back to get it' [Deuteronomy 24:19], and 'you shall not reap your field to its very border' [Leviticus 19:9]. She began to thresh, and he said: 'Give me the heave-offering, and the first and second tithe.' She accepted the ordinance and gave them all to him. What did the poor woman then do? She sold her field, and bought two sheep, to clothe herself from their fleece and to have profit from their young. When they bore their young, Aaron [i.e., the demands of the priesthood] came and said: 'Give me the first-born.' So she accepted the decision, and gave them to him. When the shearing time came, and she sheared them, Aaron came and said: 'Give me the first of the fleece of the sheep' [Deuteronomy 18:4]. Then she thought: 'I cannot stand up against this man. I will slaughter the sheep and eat them.' Then Aaron came and said: 'Give me the shoulder and the two cheeks and the stomach' [Deuteronomy 18:4]. Then she said: 'Even when I have killed them I am not safe from you. Behold they shall be *devoted*' [that is, offered to God—Ed.]. Then Aaron said: 'In that case they belong entirely to me' [Numbers 18:14].

> He took them and went away and left her weeping with her two daughters." The story is a parable of the continuous demands that the law made upon people in every action and activity of life. These demands were indeed a burden.[1]

When I read that, *I feel tired. Exhausted.* And it's not the kind of weariness that a good night's sleep will fix. And yet, Jesus spoke to people who labored under the weight of performance standards they couldn't meet. A faith that should have boosted their spirits was grinding them into the ground. The images of this text call to mind the words of Christ in this same Gospel when He says of the scribes and Pharisees, "They tie up heavy, cumbersome loads and put them on other people's shoulders" (Matthew 23:4, NIV). And the continual strain created by trying to measure up in order to find rest and peace with God was crushing people.

Had you asked them, "Are you tired, *physically* tired?" they would probably have said, "No." Had you asked them, "Are you tired of trying to be good, trying to do the right thing?" more than likely, they would have said, "Oh, yes. Pleasing

God really gets us down. We can *never* do it all." And if they answered that way, they wouldn't be the last ones to give that reply.

It is to people such as these that Jesus speaks in Matthew 11. Though He invites *anyone* to come to Him—after all, the text says, "*All* you who are weary and burdened"—He does not primarily address the physically weary or the sin sick. No, He primarily addresses well-intentioned people who are striving to do their best, and who, because of that, are exhausted and defeated. And to those people He has three words to say: "Come to Me."

Reader, are you a good person, trying to live a good life? To you, Christ says, "Come to Me." Are you doing the right things, trying hard to be a good moral person? To you, Christ says, "Come to Me." In the midst of all the good things you do, are you tired? To you, Christ says, "Come to Me." To the obligation bound, the constraint compelled, Jesus has an invitation, "Come to Me." Christ is trying to turn our hearts in a different direction.

You see, the life that is focused on the rules has one word at its core: *performance*. Before you can rest, you have to perform. And the problem is that so many of those duties are impossible to perform acceptably. So we start off defeated. But then, in an attempt to make up some ground, we focus on our outer behavior and have the tendency to just keep adding things that we were never expected to do.

On the other hand, the renewed life of which Christ speaks is a life that has a different word at the core. That word? *Person.* The experience to which Christ calls us is not *performance* based but *Person* based. He didn't say, "Come to obey," "Come to comply," "Come to perform," or "Come to fulfill." No, He said, "Come to *Me.*" Why could He say that? He could say, "Come to Me," because He also said, "*I* came to fulfill the law. And since *I* came to fulfill, *you* come to *Me*" (see Matthew 5:17).

When the dos and don'ts get you down, maybe it's time to ask yourself a simple question: What word best describes my relationship with God—*performance* or *Person*?

The way to have a *Person* at the core of our lives is to come to Jesus. And when we come to Jesus, our motivation moves from *performance* based to *Person* based, from *have to* to *want to,* from *rules* to *relationship,* from *work* to *rest.*

What exactly does that mean? *How* can I come to Him, a Person whom I cannot see? Accepting Christ's invitation involves two things, according to our text. First, He says, "Take My yoke." What does it mean to take the yoke of Christ?

The yoke was an instrument of service. It was made for the neck of oxen, made to allow them to pull a load together. But it was more than that. From ancient times, a yoke became a sign of submission, especially to a conqueror. A victorious general would mount a yoke on two spears and then make the defeated enemy army march under it as a token of submission. To "pass under the yoke" was a common expression designating submission and servitude. So when we come to Jesus, when we take His yoke, we submit to Him, live in service to Him. And in that there is rest.

"My yoke is easy," Jesus says. Another way to translate that would be to say that it is well fitting. In other words, a good yoke is one that is so carefully shaped that there will be a minimum of chafing or discomfort. *That's* the kind of yoke Jesus offers.

In Christ's day, "ox-yokes were made of wood; the ox was brought, and the measurements were taken. The yoke was then roughed out, and then the ox was brought back to have the yoke tried on. The yoke was carefully adjusted, so that it would fit well, and not chafe the neck of the patient animal. The yoke was tailor-made to fit the ox."[2] In the same way, when you come to Jesus, He makes a life of submission and service just for you.

An old legend tells that when He was a carpenter, "Jesus made the best ox-yokes in all of Galilee, and that from all over the country people came to him to buy the best yokes that skill could make. In those days, as now, shops had their signs above the doors; and it has been suggested that the sign above the door of the carpenter's shop in Nazareth may well have been: 'My yokes fit well.' "[3]

One has to wonder if Jesus, in this invitation in Matthew, uses a picture from His days in the carpenter's shop in Nazareth?

So, to take His yoke means to live in submission to His will, to carry out His direction in our daily lives in the way in which we were created.

How can I come to Him? First, I take His yoke; I submit to His will. Second, Jesus says, "Learn from Me."

T. W. Manson and Douglas Hare make the following point:

> As a designation for his *disciples* Jesus selected an Aramaic word that meant not "pupils" but "apprentices." From him they were to learn not merely to *think* but to *do.* They were to learn not only by *listening* but by *watching.* [Thus,] . . . the metaphor of the yoke attains a new force. The yoke is not one that Jesus imposes but one he wears! We remember that commonly a yoke was a wooden instrument that yoked two oxen together and made of them a team. In this word Jesus may be saying: "Become my yoke mate, and learn how to pull the load by working beside me and watching how I do it."[4]

For us today this means that we follow, observe, and listen to Christ through His Word. We take time daily, through the reading and study of His Word, to ponder His lessons, to follow His footsteps, and to observe His life. We commit His words to memory; we muse over the parables He taught; we peer deeply into the experiences of every step of His life. And, as we do so, we learn deep lessons from the One to whom we have apprenticed ourselves.

Is Jesus the high point of your life? He wants to be. In fact, there is nothing that excites Him more than the prospect of you and Him going deeper. Believe it or not, He needs you. And if you're tired of rushing through the motions of life, it may be dawning on your weary soul that you need Him too.

Play a word-association game with me. It strikes me that when I hear the word *marriage,* the first word that pops into my mind is *Anita*—the name of my wife. So let me ask, What is the first word that comes into your mind when you hear the word *religion*?

I've got some bad news, some worse news, and then I have some *very good* news. The bad news is this: if I say the word *religion* and the first word you think of is *performance,* you're in for a long, hot summer. The worse news is this: for way too many of us, the summer is in full swing.

And the good news? What is the *very* good news? Here it is. Jesus invites you to come. He says, "Come to Me." If you respond and come to Him, if you submit to and learn from Him, if you live your life by abiding in Him, then next time you hear the word *religion,* just one word will flash into your mind. One word. *Jesus.*

And when Jesus is at the heart of your life and your religion, you will know true rest.

Randy Roberts is Senior Pastor of the Loma Linda Seventh-day Adventist Church in Loma Linda, California.

---

1. William Barclay, *The Gospel of Matthew,* The New Daily Study Bible (Louisville, Ky.: Westminster John Knox Press, 2001), vol. 2, 19, 20.

2. Ibid., 20.

3. Ibid., 20.

4. T. W. Manson, *The Teaching of Jesus* (New York: Cambridge University Press, 1967), 239, 240, cited in Douglas R. A. Hare, *Matthew: Interpretation, a Bible Commentary for Preaching and Teaching* (Louisville, Ky.: Westminster John Knox Press, 2009), 128, 129; emphasis added.

Chapter 6

Love Never Ends

Experiencing God's Assurance

Elizabeth Talbot

"He did what any husband would have done for his wife," reported an online news service,[1] recounting an emotional event that took place on January 13, 2012, as the *Costa Concordia* cruise ship was sinking off the west coast of Italy. When Francis Servel and his wife, Nicole, realized that the ship was going down and the lifeboats were virtually impossible to lower, they decided to jump into the water. However, not enough life jackets were available on the cruise liner; they only had one between the two of them. Francis was a strong swimmer; he handed the life jacket to his wife and said, "Swim ahead, darling, I'll survive."[2] She never saw him again.

The whole world was stunned when the luxury cruise ship, carrying more than four thousand passengers, went down in a terrible tragedy that left many dead, several injured, and hundreds emotionally scarred for life. But it is in the midst of such a crisis that real love reveals its true colors. Self-sacrificing love is willing to give up one's life for that of another. Francis gave his life so that his wife of forty years could live. "I owe my life to my husband," said the now heartbroken Mrs. Servel.[3] And she does. It is only real love that makes the ultimate sacrifice. When disaster strikes, instances of people giving their lives for their loved ones remind us that the human heart still carries the image of its Creator deep within.

How could God demonstrate the magnitude and scope of His love for us? How could He communicate the depth, width, and strength of His love for a fallen race, when the noblest values and displays of human feeling don't even come close to expressing it? Well, He decided to use the love of a husband for his wife and of parents for their child—the two deepest bonds of love that exist on this earth—to give us a glimpse of His love for us. These two metaphors are used throughout the Bible to unveil the passion of a God who loved us more than Himself, and ultimately gave up His life for His people, who had rejected Him. In this chapter, we will marvel at God's plan to save His people with the passion of a Lover who willingly surrenders His own life for His beloved bride. The words keep ringing in my ears as if Jesus were saying them to me: "Go ahead, darling. I'll catch up"; and He went to the cross and died in my place, giving me His own life jacket, that I may now have the assurance of eternal life. But let's start this love story from the beginning, shall we?

The beginning

"In the beginning God created the heavens and the earth" (Genesis 1:1).[4] The seven Hebrew words that initiate this love story foreshadow the seven days of Creation. God, who is love and exists in the selfless intimate community of Three Persons in One, was about to create humankind—a race to love and cherish. As a passionate Lover awaiting the love of His life, He designed the most beautiful place, the earth, which He filled with animals and beautiful plants, providing exquisite scents and colorful flowers for His beloved to enjoy. After each day of creative work, He whispered to Himself words of approval: things were going well as He prepared for the arrival of His beloved.

From the second day on, you can almost envision God rubbing His hands together in excitement as He looked around and concluded that "it was good" (verses 10, 12, 18, 21, 25). All through the week He kept creating beauty and kept saying, "It's good; it's good; it's good!"

I was arriving home from one of my frequent weekend preaching trips. It was evening and I was tired and ready to go to sleep after a long flight. But when I entered the dining room, I saw something that totally took my tiredness (and breath) away, which I will never forget. My husband, Patrick, had created an exquisite composition on the dining table that profusely communicated his love for me. The table was covered with a square red cloth; on it, there was a large heart design made of many tiny hearts. Underlining the beautiful heart, he had placed two large fine chocolates, wrapped in shiny paper. I was so utterly touched! And he also gave me a bouquet of gorgeous roses. I was speechless! My husband had managed to powerfully communicate his love for me, not only through the beautiful and thoughtful composition itself but also through the fact that he had spent so much time and effort and invested so much creativity in forming this beautiful atmosphere, just to let me know how much I mean to him! Thank you, Patrick, I am still so touched! Well, that's the type of endearing planning that I see in the Creation week, highlighted by the details in its biblical account. God is designing and planning every plant and flower for His loved ones. Even though they don't exist yet, He is already busy crafting beautiful things just for them!

And then the day arrived! God paused for the only "divine dialogue" that we read of in the Creation account: "Then God said, 'Let us make man in our image, according to our likeness.' . . . God created man in His own image, in the image of God He created him; male and female He created them" (verses 26, 27). The beloved had arrived! And when they did, they found a most beautiful place created just for them! That day was not only good like the others. Oh, no! That day was "*very good*"! (verse 31; emphasis added). He had planted a special Garden for His beloved. It was so beautiful that in the Greek translation of the Hebrew Scriptures (the Old Testament), which was used by the New Testament writers, the word chosen for this Garden is *paradeisos* (Genesis 2:8). It was so beautiful that it was *Paradise*! He placed a special tree in the middle of Paradise to remind the couple that they were designed to stay in intimacy with Him forever! This tree was called the tree of life, and it reminded them that they were immortal.

God wanted to give humans the capacity to love selflessly, too, so that they might understand His love better. And because God exists in the intimate community that we call the Trinity, He intended that a woman and a man also would exist in an intimate community that we call marriage: "For this reason a man shall leave his father and his mother, and be joined to his wife; and they shall become one flesh" (verse 24). I think it is extremely important and revealing that the Hebrew word used for "one" in this verse is the same word used in the *Shema* when describing the "oneness" of God: "Hear, O Israel! The Lord is our God, the Lord is one!" (Deuteronomy 6:4). The *Shema* (Hebrew for "hear"), found in Deuteronomy 6:4–9, is the Jewish confession of faith, to be recited daily. God is one God, existing in community, as a man and a woman are one flesh. Perhaps now humankind would understand God's selfless love for them a little bit better.

I would like to tell you that God and His beloved lived happily ever after in that beautiful Paradise created just for them. I would love to tell you that this is the end of the love story. But I can't. This is only the beginning. The ship would sink, the race would fall, and the beloved would go down into the depths of sin. But as I said before, it is in the midst of a crisis that real love reveals its true colors.

The crisis

As any person who is in love would tell you, you can't hold your beloved hostage. Love simply can't exist without freedom; therefore, freedom to choose is a basic prerequisite for love to exist. If freedom is not in the equation, then love is turned into fear. That's why, aside from the tree that reminded them of God's eternal plan (the tree of life), there was another tree; it was called the tree of the knowledge of good and evil (Genesis 2:9). If they ever wanted to leave God and His moral umbrella, this was their way out. Genesis 3 tells the saddest story known to humankind: the day the beloved left, going after new enticing possibilities, blinded by an exotic and beautiful tempter and his promises of "more" to come—just like adulterous hearts today. Their senses were aroused and an anticipation of the forbidden delight overcame them:

> When the woman saw that the tree was good for food, and that it was a delight to the eyes, and that the tree was desirable to make one wise, she took from its fruit and ate; and she gave also to her husband with her, and he ate. Then the eyes of both of them were opened, and they knew that they were naked; and they sewed fig leaves together and made themselves loin coverings (Genesis 3:6, 7).

The grass always looks greener on the other side—until you are there! For the first time, they realized the shame of their unfaithfulness to the Creator. Even though they had been naked before without shame (Genesis 2:25), now they knew evil and they felt the need to cover their nakedness (Genesis 3:7). God came looking for His beloved in the Garden (verse 8), but this time they hid instead of running toward Him! Fear, shame, and blame followed (verses 9–13). What would happen now? Were they doomed forever? They deserved it! They had brought it upon themselves! They were in deep, cold waters. The ship had sunk, and they had no life jackets! They were dying, and they knew it! And it was their entire fault! But then they heard the voice of their Beloved: "Go ahead, darling, I'll catch up."

The life jacket

A lover does not give up easily, and neither did God. When the crisis arose, He spoke to the serpent in the presence of Adam and Eve. He announced that this was not the end, that even if He had to die for them, He would not give up! This is the first assurance of love in the Bible: "I will put enmity between you and the woman, and between your seed and her seed; he shall bruise you on the head, and you shall bruise him on the heel" (verse 15). God had a plan; He threw the only life jacket to His *beloved.* Even though they would be separated temporarily because the humans were now mortal and had lost the *paradeisos* (verse 24), God would take their death upon Himself, so that they could be together again—forever. He simply refused to go through eternity without His people, His cherished bride.

He would not only be their Creator but also their Redeemer. He would "swim" in their place, and He would die in the process. And this brings us to one of the most fascinating themes in the Scriptures: the *go'el.* I truly believe that once we understand this concept, which is present from Genesis to Revelation, we will start to comprehend the plan of salvation. *Go'el* is a Hebrew word meaning "kinsman-redeemer." The "closest of kin" could do several things for his beloved relative that no one else could do. For example, the *go'el* could redeem a relative who had sold himself into slavery (Leviticus 25:47–54). He could set him or her free! Also, the *go'el* could redeem property that was given up by a poor relative (verses 25–34). And the *go'el* was the one who would marry the widow of a close relative who had died without descendants in order to provide for the widow and to ensure that the family lineage was not interrupted, thus removing the shame from the kin. The book of Ruth is written with this concept in mind. (Take a few minutes to read it; it is a fascinating love story!) When Naomi and Ruth became widows and returned to Bethlehem as two destitute women, they discovered that Boaz was their *go'el* (Ruth 2:20), and they rejoiced.

Eventually, Ruth asked him to take her under his protection and provision: "I am Ruth your maid. So spread your covering over your maid, for you are a close relative [*go'el*]" (Ruth 3:9). He did, and Ruth's shame was taken away. He became her redeemer.

When God created us in His image, He pledged Himself to a rescue plan because He was our "closest of kin." He is our *go'el,* and we are His beloved. This word becomes a descriptive name for God in the Scriptures, usually translated as "Redeemer" in our Bibles (Isaiah 63:16). When Jesus became flesh, He fulfilled all the roles of the *go'el,* giving His life for our ransom, redeeming us, not with money but with His blood (Mark 10:45; Isaiah 52:3), as well as redeeming our land. This is the most amazing theme running throughout the Scriptures. It explains that when we trust in the ransom paid by our *go'el,* we can live with the assurance of eternal life. "I know that my Redeemer lives" (Job 19:25)! Oh, my dear Beloved, spread your covering over me—and take my shame away.

Happily ever after

He gave us His life jacket, died in our place, and took our shame away! Even at the very moment of His death, He reminded His beloved that, in spite of the unfaithfulness of humankind, the way to *paradeisos* was being reopened. Jesus' promise to the evildoer at the cross, who had requested Christ to remember him, reads, "You shall be with Me in Paradise" (Luke 23:43). This is the only record of Jesus using the word *paradeisos* in His ministry on earth. And He used it at the appropriate time! "Go ahead, darling, I'll catch up." Yes! Paradise! Remember? We will be back together forever!

The assurance of our future rests in His sacrificial love at the cross. When I need confidence about my eternal life, I must look back to the moment when God reopened Paradise for His people. At that moment, the assurance given in Genesis 3:15 became a reality, and now our *go'el* is coming back for His bride. Will you join us for this marriage feast? "Let us rejoice and be glad and give the glory to Him, for the marriage of the Lamb has come and His bride has made herself ready" (Revelation 19:7). Our *go'el,* who gave us His life jacket, who died in our place and was resurrected, is now coming back. I can't wait for that hug after all these years! He is eager to embrace us: "Yes, I am coming quickly"

(Revelation 22:20). Yes! Our Beloved is coming back to take us home. REJOICE!

Woo-Hoo!

Elizabeth Talbot is Speaker/Director of the Jesus101 Biblical Institute, Simi Valley, California.

---

1. "Costa Concordia Cruise Disaster: Husband Sacrifices Life Jacket for Wife, Disappears Into Water," *Huffington Post,* January 16, 2012, accessed April 5, 2012, http://www.huffingtonpost.com/2012/01/16/costa-concordia-cruise-disaster_n_1208773.html.

2. "Swim Ahead, Darling, I'll Survive: 'My Husband Gave Me His Lifejacket as We Jumped Off Sinking Cruise Ship . . . I Never Saw Him Again,' Says French Survivor," *Daily Mail,* January 19, 2012, accessed April 5, 2012, http://www.dailymail.co.uk/news/article-2086826/Costa-Concordia-cruise-ship-accident-French-survivor-tells-husband-gave-lifejacket.html. Nicole Servel reported that Francis told her, "Go on my darling, swim straight ahead. I will get myself out." The newspaper condensed his words into, "Swim ahead, darling, I'll survive" to fit the space.

3. Ibid.

4. All Bible quotations in this chapter are from the New American Standard Bible.

Chapter 7

The Comeback

Experiencing God's Hope

Carlton P. Byrd

The year was 1995. The place was the famous Madison Square Garden in New York City. The setting was game 1 of the National Basketball Association (NBA) Eastern Conference Semifinals between the New York Knicks and the Indiana Pacers. Knicks fans loathed Indiana Pacers star guard Reggie Miller so much that ESPN made this game the subject of one of their *30 for 30* documentaries.[1] To the disdain of loyal Knicks fans, Miller single-handedly led his team to a stunning 107–105 comeback win over the Knicks in the Garden.

With 18.7 seconds left in the game, the Knicks led by six points. Miller then made a three-pointer, stole the ensuing inbounds pass, dribbled behind the three-point line, and made another three-pointer. Miller later made two free throws to put the Pacers ahead for the win and up 1–0 in the series. This is considered by many as one of the greatest comebacks in NBA history. This is a sports comeback.

After nine years of combat in Iraq, the last American soldiers left Iraq in December 2011. The soldiers have made a comeback home. When they enter airports, people cheer! When they walk down city streets, people smile and nod in respect and appreciation. Our soldiers have come back! This is a physical comeback.

The Bible also talks about comebacks. In Luke 15:11–32, Jesus tells the parable of the "comeback," the parable of the prodigal son. A father has two sons. The younger son demands his inheritance early and leaves home. The older son remains at home and works.

The younger son spends his money on "riotous," foolish living. He then reaches his lowest point. He feeds on what pigs would eat. He later comes to himself and decides he's going home to his father. He would do better in his father's house as a servant.

As the son walks up the long driveway to his father's house, his father sees him in the distance.

His father shouts in excitement and brings him the best robe! He says, "Let's have a feast! This, my son, was lost and is now found! He was blind, but now he sees."

This parable illustrates that when you come back to our heavenly Father, He receives you with open, outstretched arms and says, "Come back home." This is a spiritual comeback.

But the ultimate comeback will not be when the Pacers beat the Knicks. Neither will it be when the American troops or prodigals return back home. The greatest comeback will be when the trumpet sounds and Jesus comes back in the clouds!

The Bible describes Jesus' comeback like this: "The Lord Himself will descend from heaven with a shout, with the voice of an archangel, and with the trumpet of God. And the dead in Christ shall rise first. Then we who are alive and remain shall be caught up together with them in the clouds to meet the Lord in the air. And thus we shall always be with the Lord" (1 Thessalonians 4:16, 17).[2]

This is the ultimate comeback—the second coming of Jesus Christ! This is our eternal hope! This is our eternal desire! Jesus is coming back!

There will be no more crying, dying, sickness, cancer, arthritis, high blood pressure, high gas prices, house mortgages, car payments, trials, tears, or tests! The former things are going to pass away, and all things are going to become new (Revelation 21:4)! Jesus is going to make a comeback! This is our blessed hope!

Approximately two thousand years ago, Jesus returned to heaven to be with God the Father. Just prior to His ascension, however, the bewildered disciples asked Him, "Lord, will You at this time restore the kingdom to Israel?" (Acts 1:6). Mistakenly, the disciples thought that Jesus was going to initiate His kingdom and rule at that time. The disciples didn't understand the nature of Christ's kingdom. Jesus had not promised the sort of restoration they were anticipating.

In response to their question, Christ did not give a specific, direct answer. But instead, He directed them to the work that lay ahead. He gave them instructions to coincide with the great gospel commission of Matthew 28:19, 20. He said, "Go therefore and make disciples of all the nations, baptizing them in the name of the Father and of the Son and of the Holy Spirit, teaching them to observe all things that I have commanded you; and lo, I am with you always, even to the end of the age" (Matthew 28:19, 20).

He then promised in Acts 1 that He would not leave the disciples feeling abandoned because He was sending them the Holy Spirit! "You shall receive power when the Holy Spirit has come upon you: and you shall be witnesses to Me in Jerusalem, and in all Judea and Samaria, and to the end of the earth" (Acts 1:8).

In short, Jesus told His disciples to get ready, for the Holy Spirit was going to act. Get ready, for the gospel is going to be preached! The sick will be healed! The dead will be raised! The blind will see! Miracles will be wrought! And thousands will be baptized in the name of the Father, the Son, and the Holy Spirit! Disciples, don't be discouraged; power will be transferred to you!

"When He had spoken these things, while they watched, He was taken up, and a cloud received Him out of their sight" (verse 9). What a magnificent sight this must have been! Can you imagine the ascension of Jesus back to His Father?

Jesus, in whom they had believed,

Jesus, in whom they had witnessed the manifestation of miracles,

Jesus, who had died on the cross,

Jesus, who had rested in a tomb, but was raised from the dead by the power of God, was now taken up, and a cloud received Him out of their sight!

"While they looked steadfastly toward heaven as He went up, behold, two men stood by them in white apparel, who also said, 'Men of Galilee, why do you stand gazing up into heaven? This same Jesus, who was taken up from you into heaven, will so come in like manner as you saw Him go into heaven' " (verses 10, 11).

In other words, the angels said, "Don't be afraid. This same Jesus is going to make a comeback just like He left. Don't worry. Don't fret. Jesus is leaving now, but He's coming back!"

And His comeback will be personal: "This same Jesus."

It will be visible: We "saw Him go."

It will be with clouds: "A cloud received Him."

It will be certain: "This same Jesus . . . will so come in like manner as you saw Him go."

This is what the life of the Christian is all about—looking forward to Jesus' comeback, Jesus' second coming! And while we don't know the exact date of the comeback, we do know that it will be soon. We know this because the Bible tells us the signs and events in earth's history that will take place just prior to Jesus' coming.

Matthew 24:3–14, 36–39 specifically gives us this information:

> Now as He sat on the Mount of Olives, the disciples came to Him privately, saying, "Tell us, when will these things be? And what will be the sign of Your coming, and of the end of the age?" And Jesus answered and said to them: "Take heed that no one deceives you. For many will come in My name, saying, 'I am the Christ,' and will deceive many. And you will hear of wars and rumors of wars. See that you are not troubled; for all these things must come to pass, but the end is not yet. For nation will rise against nation, and kingdom against kingdom. And there will be famines, pestilences, and earthquakes in various places. All these are the beginning of sorrows. Then they will deliver you up to tribulation and kill you, and you will be hated by all nations for My name's sake. And then many will be offended, will betray one

> another, and will hate one another. Then many false prophets will rise up and deceive many. And because lawlessness will abound, the love of many will grow cold. But he who endures to the end shall be saved. And this gospel of the kingdom will be preached in all the world as a witness to all the nations, and then the end will come. . . .
>
> "But of that day and hour no one knows, not even the angels of heaven, but My Father only. But as the days of Noah were, so also will the coming of the Son of Man be. For as in the days before the flood, they were eating and drinking, marrying and giving in marriage, until the day that Noah entered the ark, and did not know until the flood came and took them all away, so also will the coming of the Son of Man be."

War, poverty, death, disease, and destruction are all prevalent in our world today. What was outlined in Matthew 24 is being witnessed in our present world.

Our hope rests in knowing that Jesus is going to make a comeback soon. And although we don't know the exact date of His coming, we need to always be ready. "Watch therefore, for you do not know what hour your Lord is coming. . . . Therefore you also be ready, for the Son of Man is coming at an hour you do not expect" (verses 42, 44). So though we don't know with certainty when He's coming, we do know with surety that when Jesus comes back, it will be in the same manner in which He left. He left in a cloud, and He will return in a cloud. He left in the air, and He will return in the air.

Revelation 1:7 also teaches us that when He makes His comeback every living "eye will see Him." Hence, those in North America will see Him! Those in South America will see Him! Those in Africa will see Him! Those in Antarctica will see Him! Those in Asia will see Him! Those in Australia will see Him! Those in Europe will see Him! We will all see Him, and see Him at the same time! "Behold, He is coming with clouds, and every eye will see Him" (verse 7).

Christ's second coming will be a glorious event! It will be an exciting time of union with Christ and reunion with family and friends who have died in Christ! We have been given this promise: "The Lord Himself will descend from heaven with a shout, with the voice of an archangel, and with the trumpet of God. And the dead in Christ will rise first. Then we who are alive and remain shall be caught up together with them in the clouds to meet the Lord in the air. And thus we shall always be with the Lord" (1 Thessalonians 4:16, 17).

It will also be an exciting time because we will be changed! We will have new bodies! We will have new minds! We will have new schedules!

> Behold, I tell you a mystery: We shall not all sleep, but we shall all be changed—in a moment, in the twinkling of an eye, at the last trumpet. For the trumpet will sound, and the dead will be raised incorruptible, and we shall be changed. For this corruptible must put on incorruption, and this mortal must put on immortality. So when this corruptible has put on incorruption, and this mortal has put on immortality, then shall be brought to pass the saying that is written: "Death is swallowed up in victory." "O Death, where is your sting? O Hades, where is your victory?" The sting of death is sin, and the strength of sin is the law. But thanks be to God, who gives us the victory through our Lord Jesus Christ.

> Therefore, my beloved brethren, be steadfast, immovable, always abounding in the work of the Lord, knowing that your labor is not in vain in the Lord (1 Corinthians 15:51–58).

What a blessed hope! What an encouraging hope! What a certain hope! As Christ's modern-day disciples, we have nothing to fear or fret. Our current state of affairs will not last forever. Jesus is coming back just as He said He would! And this hope is not a sports comeback. This hope is not a physical comeback. This hope is not an individualized spiritual comeback. But this hope lies in Jesus Christ's comeback.

The first time Jesus came to this earth He came to *save* His people! "She will bring forth a Son, and you shall call His name Jesus, for He will save His people from their sins" (Matthew 1:21). When Jesus makes His comeback at the Second Coming, He's coming back to *get* His people! "Let not your heart be troubled; you believe in God, believe also in Me. In My Father's house are many mansions; if it were not so, I would have told you. I go to prepare a place for you. And if I go and prepare a place for you, I will come again and receive you to Myself; that where I am, there you may be also" (John 14:1–3). Praise God for this hope!

We have this hope that burns within our hearts.
Hope in the coming of the Lord!
We have this faith that Christ alone imparts.
Faith in the promise of His Word!
We believe the time is near, when the nations far and near,
shall awake and shout and sing, "Hallelujah! Christ is King!"
We have this hope that burns within our hearts!
Hope in the coming of the Lord![3]

Carlton P. Byrd is Speaker/Director of the Breath of Life *television broadcast and Senior Pastor of the Oakwood University Seventh-day Adventist Church.*

---

1. *Winning Time: Reggie Miller vs. the New York Knicks,* directed by Dan Klores, *30 for 30* series (Bristol, Conn.: ESPN Films, 2010), DVD.

2. Unless otherwise noted, all Scripture quotations in this chapter are from the New King James Version.

3. Wayne Hooper, "We Have This Hope," in *The Seventh-day Adventist Hymnal* (Hagerstown, Md.: Review and Herald® Publishing Association, 1985), hymn no. 214.

Chapter 8

One Sign You Don't Want to Miss

Experiencing God's Leading

José Vicente Rojas

Then certain of the scribes and of the Pharisees answered, saying, Master, we would see a sign from thee. But he answered and said unto them, An evil and adulterous generation seeketh after a sign; and there shall no sign be given to it, but the sign of the prophet [Jonah.]

—Matthew 12:38–40[1]

They had spent the long day along the shores of Galilee. Jesus had healed hundreds of people of their diseases throughout the morning and had preached for several hours into the evening. Because of the huge crowds, Jesus got into a boat and pushed out a few yards from the shore, a technique that had helped Him speak to large gatherings at other times. Many natural acoustic settings existed in Galilee, including a cove near Capernaum that would enable thousands to hear the voice of a person who stood in just the right place.

You would think that by the end of the sermon, Jesus was ready to go home to rest, but the crowd still needed Him. As He got off the boat, Jesus told His disciples that the people needed to eat. The disciples responded that Jesus was asking the impossible, for there was not enough food to distribute to five thousand men, in addition to women and children.

After a disciple found a young boy carrying a lunch basket that his mother had prepared, containing five loaves of bread and two little fish, Jesus gave instructions for everyone in the crowd to sit in groups of fifty and a hundred. After blessing the food, Jesus proceeded to break the loaves and fishes, and the disciples distributed the food to the people. Everyone ate a full supper that evening from the miraculously multiplied bread and fish, with enough left over to take home to family and friends!

When they approached Him with their request, the religious leaders had no doubt witnessed many similar days during which Jesus had taught and healed and cast out demons and supplied the people's needs. This puzzling encounter is recorded in Matthew 12:38–40: "Then certain of the scribes and of the Pharisees answered, saying, Master, we would see a sign from thee. But he answered and said unto them, An evil and adulterous generation seeketh after a sign; and there shall no sign be given to it, but the sign of the prophet Jonas [Jonah]."

How can it be possible that highly educated men could make this incredible request after having watched Jesus over the weeks and months as He performed miracle after miracle? Hadn't these leaders seen Jesus healing countless numbers of people? Hadn't they heard Him preach of His Father's kingdom?

Jesus said to His disciples on several occasions that many, "Seeing, do not see"; He also said, "Many, hearing, do not hear" (see Matthew 13:13). Is it possible to hear Jesus speak and see Jesus perform miracles, without ever understanding the enormity of what He's done to lead us? Because the religious leaders were expecting a military Messiah, they could not perceive the Divine Messiah among them. Over and over in the Gospels, Jesus does not conform to human views of salvation. Instead, Jesus calls on us to follow Him, and He does the work of transforming us into His image.

Jesus' strong response to the request for a sign comes across as an expression of deep sadness. Jesus probably spoke with tear-filled eyes as He informed the leadership from Jerusalem that this adulterous generation would not receive a sign, except the sign of the prophet Jonah.

The story of Jonah was well known in Israel. Most people were aware of the great calling Jonah received from God to go to Nineveh and warn its inhabitants of the consequences of sin that were to befall their city. The sins of Nineveh had reached a point of such extreme depravity that the only solution was for God to destroy the city. But God in His love sought to save the people of Nineveh, so He sent Jonah on a mission of mercy.

Jonah feared his mission at first and fled in the opposite direction from Nineveh. He boarded a ship bound for Tarsus. While on the seas, a violent storm threatened to sink the ship, and all on board knew they would likely perish that night. Jonah realized the blessing of God was not with him. When we flee from God, it is not God who takes away His blessing. Instead, we are the ones who choose to turn our backs and walk away from God's blessing!

The Bible tells us that Jonah requested to be thrown overboard, promising that if the sailors did this, the storm would end. When the desperate crew tossed Jonah into the violent seas—immediately after he splashed into the water—the storm calmed and the seas became still. A giant fish swimming by broke the surface with a big splash, swallowed Jonah, then quickly and silently disappeared into the depths. For the next three difficult days, Jonah was carried in the belly of that giant fish and was finally deposited by the fish onto the shore outside the city of Nineveh.

Think for a moment about what this story meant to the culture of the people of Israel. This story is an example of God's mercy and love for His people. In the account of what befell the people of Sodom and Gomorrah, God took the unprecedented step of reaching out to them. Through Abraham and Lot, God pleaded with the people of those two great cities to choose life rather than continuing on the path toward destruction, where they were headed. Many people don't understand that the historical accounts of

Sodom and Gomorrah, like the story of Nineveh, are stories of God's mercy, of God going the extra mile to warn His people! This is another biblical example of what is referred to as "the gospel," the good news of God.

In our world we see many natural disasters. Through the years I have personally experienced earthquakes, floods, hurricanes, mountain fires, tornadoes, hailstorms, windstorms, blizzards, droughts, and other natural disasters. Each of these disasters, and many others, destroy thousands of lives every year. But for some of these natural disasters, science has now found a way to accurately predict the level of the disaster and the approximate time of its arrival. This is very good news for our society.

Because of these scientific advancements, local governments can now issue warnings so that citizens can prepare and evacuate from the path of the natural disaster. Each year, by issuing early warnings, countless people have been saved from certain death in many places. Only a few decades ago, a hurricane could suddenly level an entire city and its population. Now, because of warning systems, people are able to evacuate early, so when the storm strikes, few are there to suffer its destruction. Thank God for the good news of warnings!

A warning from God is a wonderful thing. When God reaches out to His people and informs us of the deadly disasters of sin swirling about us, we can be thankful for that kind of love. When God issues warnings, they are not intended to cause us to look at Him as a stern God. Instead, we have the opportunity to look deeper into the eyes of a loving God who, in a timely way, tells us what is to come so that no one can say, "I didn't know!"

When Jonah preached in Nineveh, a miracle happened. Nineveh was different from Sodom and Gomorrah. By the end of Jonah's first sermon, beginning with the king of Nineveh, the people repented of their sins and turned to the Lord. So great was the response of the people of Nineveh that a revival took place. One of the blessings of discipleship with Jesus is that true revival always leads to transformation. When we come to a personal realization of how much our sin separates us from God and we experience true forgiveness, we are not only revived in our faith, we are also on a path of transformation. God literally changes our lives!

Israel was aware for centuries that when the people of Nineveh repented of their sins, leading God to spare their city, Jonah became angry. Jonah had preferred to see the destruction of Nineveh rather than salvation for the people. Jonah had thought his calling was to condemn the city. But God demonstrated to Jonah that the good news of mercy and salvation were the reasons for his calling. Jonah had gone to warn the city and to call its inhabitants to repentance. The people heeded the warning and were blessed with life.

Sadly, many people today seem to think that God has called us to condemn the world. A famous sermon preached in 1741 was titled "Sinners in the Hands of an Angry God." Later put into print, this sermon detailed the brutal agony the author imagined that most of humanity will suffer when God supposedly has His retribution on the earth. The sermon described flames and torture as sinners felt forever the actual pain in hell. The sermon is said to have had a huge effect on people in the United States, mainly because readers were shocked and terrified into "going to church."

Like Jonah, some would actually prefer to see the deaths of billions of people because of the sin problem on earth. This idea of retribution for sin is still in the minds of those who don't understand the meaning of true discipleship. While God does hate sin, never forget that God loves the sinner! To carry the warning of God to others today is actually the joy of extending the good news of God's mercy to a dying world.

As Jesus looked into the unbelieving eyes of the religious leaders who had asked for another miracle after having witnessed many, He sought to make clear to them that repentance leads to forgiveness, placing anyone who responds on the path of salvation. One of the greatest obstacles was that Israel's religious leaders had come to publicly categorize sin. Their own personal sins, the terrible destructive sins of pride, judgmentalism, and self-righteousness, they considered as harmless and somehow appropriate in their lives. But other sins, the sins of the common man and woman in the community, had come to be characterized as abominations in their culture.

Jesus was unequivocal that all sin separates us from God. By reminding the scribes and Pharisees of Jonah and his call to minister to Nineveh, Jesus put into context His mission to save humanity. Again Jesus would illustrate how He did not come to call the righteous but sinners to repentance.

Jesus even went as far as to tell the influential leaders that as Jonah was in the belly of the fish for three days, so also, He would be in the heart of the earth for three days. As Jonah came out of the fish after three days, leading to the salvation of Nineveh, so also Jesus would come out of the tomb after three days, leading to the salvation of humanity!

Warnings from Jesus are a great blessing. You and I can prepare for spiritual storms to come. No one needs to be caught off guard, unaware of the future. A true disciple walks with a sense of forgiveness, of belonging, with a certainty of personhood in Jesus. Just as in daily living there are warnings of impending physical dangers, so also there are warnings of spiritual dangers.

We can better understand why Jesus, in His love and mercy, has warned us of things to come. Remember that storms are most devastating to those who ignore warnings. Those who respond to warnings do not experience the worst of storms. Just talk to citizens of the Gulf States region of the

United States who respond to hurricane warnings, or people in Oklahoma who respond to tornado warnings. Ask people in California who retrofit their homes for earthquakes, or Hawaiians who respond to tsunami warnings. Ask Canadians about blizzard warnings, and the people of Idaho about fire warnings. No matter what the warning, those who respond are blessed, but those who ignore the warnings end up suffering from their choices.

We can choose life. Through warnings we confirm that in Jesus we have life everlasting and the devil will have his end. With the evidence that his time is short, we should not expect the devil to go quietly to his demise. When Jesus shouted, "It is finished!" from the cross, He really meant it. The devil knows his time is coming, and all he wants is to take as many people with him as he can. But Jesus fully paid the price for our sins and plans to take us home.

The final chapters of earth's history are before us. God is preparing now to usher in His kingdom. The sign of His leading is a wonderful call for us to respond to Him just as Nineveh did long ago. A revival and transformation led to great blessings for the people of Nineveh. A revival and transformation in our lives will have a similar effect today.

Have you seen the sign of His leading in your life? This is your opportunity to respond.

José Vincente Rojas is Director of the Office of Volunteer Ministries for the North American Division of Seventh-day Adventists.

---

1. Unless otherwise noted, all Bible quotations in this chapter are from the King James Version.

Chapter 9

Take Your Stand

Experiencing God's Calling

Fred Kinsey

"Why did Jesus have to stand alone?" I asked my mother one Sabbath afternoon many years ago. We were leaving the Hall of the Crucifixion-Resurrection at Forest Lawn Cemetery in Glendale, California, where we had just viewed *The Crucifixion,* a painting by the Polish artist Jan Styka. I was probably still in elementary school at the Glendale Adventist Academy.

My earliest memories about the death of Jesus are vivid and are likely colored by the enormous painting—one of the largest on canvas ever created. Housed in a large cathedral-like building constructed especially to showcase it, the massive image depicts the moments just *before* Christ was put on the cross.

To the moving music of Richard Strauss, I remember the 45-foot tall curtain being drawn open along the 195-foot width of the image, revealing Jesus standing alone near the cross. The awful darkness that would settle over the scene has not yet taken place.

In the painting, I noticed thousands of people streaming through the gates of Jerusalem to witness the execution. Christ's accusers are there, standing off to the side. Some of Christ's disciples are there, but like His mother, Mary, they stand some distance away. Jesus stands alone, looking up into heaven.

I now recognize certain inaccuracies. Jesus does not appear to have been beaten. I don't recall a crown of thorns around His head. Still, to me the horror of horrors was that no one stood with Him.

Apparently, the artist intended to portray Jesus going through this monumental event by Himself. "My God, My God," Christ would say, "why have You forsaken Me?" quoting Psalm 22 (Matthew 27:46).[1] It was difficult enough to contemplate Jesus dying, but all the more horrible that He was doing it so alone and so publicly at the same time. A line from an old hymn comes to mind: "Must Jesus bear the cross alone, and all the world go free?"[2]

I asked my mother why no one stood with Jesus. Perhaps she didn't know what to say, but her response became a part of my life. It was one of those teachable moments every parent is granted a precious few times in life. "When you grow up," she said, "I certainly hope *you* will."

As I reflect on it now, my response to my mother was more like Peter's commitment at the Last Supper. "I *will* stand with Jesus, Mom!" I had said. Though I earnestly meant it, to be honest, like Peter, I drifted at times.

My understanding at that time was rather elementary and childlike—full of desire but not sure what to do with it. Perhaps you could say I was like the disciples. I had spent time with Jesus; but when trouble arose, my faith would be tested and, quite honestly, I often failed. I had seen a picture of Jesus and wanted to be like and be with Him. This is the first step in the transformational process that leads to being a true disciple of Jesus.

But our adversary, whom Peter describes as a "roaring lion" (1 Peter 5:8), is still ready to take a bite out of any person who wishes to commit his or her life to Jesus and stand with Him! Satan's attacks are often crafty and elegant and come at times we least expect them. That's what makes the "roaring lion" analogy so illustrative. Lions don't often roar when their prey expects an attack. They let out those nerve-shattering roars when the prey thinks it is safe. According to legend, the lion's roar often makes the attack successful because the prey is rendered defenseless by heart failure.

As I think back over my life, it seems that the greatest success the roaring lion has had with me is in pointing out how unworthy of Jesus' grace I really am. Honestly, I know it is true! It's true for all of humankind: "All have sinned and fall short of the glory of God" (Romans 3:23).

How often I've heard satanic accusations said with a sneer, "And you call yourself a Christian and *did* that?" Or, "You call yourself a Christian and *thought* that?"

Like the prey of the roaring lion, too often I've been ready to give up, but then the story of Peter's interaction with Jesus at the Last Supper comes to mind, floating like a life preserver on the rough waves of the ocean.

The true beauty of the exchange between Jesus and Peter is sometimes lost on readers because of the chapters placed in the Bible many years after it was written.

At the end of John 13, beginning in verse 36, is this conversation:

> Simon Peter asked him, "Lord, where are you going?"
>
> Jesus replied, "Where I am going, you cannot follow now, but you will follow later."
>
> Peter asked, "Lord, why can't I follow you now? I will lay down my life for you."
>
> Then Jesus answered, "Will you really lay down your life for me? Very truly I tell you, before the rooster crows, you will disown me three times!" (NIV).

Imagine Peter's feelings. He, along with the rest of the remaining disciples, has just witnessed Judas being identified as a betrayer. And when Judas leaves, the Bible says cryptically, "And it was night" (verse 30). The darkness in the room would grow figuratively denser when Jesus makes the statement, "Where I am going, you cannot come" (verse 33, NIV).

At this Peter is aghast. Someone must stand with Jesus—and it might as well be him! Before his fellow disciples Peter, in effect, declares, "You can count on me to stand with You! I will defend You with my life."

Imagine Peter's consternation at being told that he would not remain faithful through the night. "Before the rooster crows today, you will deny three times that you know me," Jesus tells him (Luke 22:34, NIV). Peter knew better than to doubt the accuracy of these words.

How like Peter we often are. We make our big pronouncements about following Christ, only to fail miserably. We are truly unworthy! The accusations are true!

For many, the story ends here, just as in the Bible as John 13 comes to a close. Like Peter, we expect no further word on the matter. We made our big proclamation, only to have our fallibility prominently displayed. But Christ stands with us despite our unworthiness and failures. It is unfortunate that the chapter break between John 13 and 14 is placed where it is. When Christ tells Peter that he won't make it through the night without denying Him multiple times, Jesus has not finished speaking!

What compassion is heard next: "Let not your heart be troubled," Jesus says. What? Jesus goes on to say that there are many dwelling places in heaven especially for people like Peter—like me! "If it were not so," Jesus adds, "I would have told you. I go to prepare a place for you" (John 14:1, 2). Jesus is preparing a place for people who can't make it through the night without denying Him flagrantly? Decidedly so!

Success in the Christian experience is not assured because we stand with Jesus, but because Jesus stands with us!

During His reassurance to Peter, Jesus reminds him, "You believe in God; believe also in me" (verse 1, NIV). Jesus requests a commitment on our part. I realize now that Christ in His great love has committed to stand with me and hopes that, in response, I won't stand away from Him! Jesus ends His discourse with Peter with the reassurance that all of us must hear: "That where I am, there you may be also" (verse 3, NASB).

Jesus wants us to be where He is! What a glorious thought!

But Jesus would not only witness His disciples forsaking Him for fear, He would also come out of the tomb without His followers waiting for Him! Didn't they remember He said something about that taking place? Had I been Jesus, I might have just given up and written off the previous three years as wasted. But Jesus comes out of the grave and almost immediately goes searching for those who not only didn't take their stand with Him, but He also specifically remembers Peter, who denied Him.

Saturday night in our secular world is often known for being "party time." But on a Saturday night many years ago, it was not a time to celebrate and revel in a good time! There was depression and discouragement.

As the disciples gathered in a nondescript room, fearing the Romans, certain questions certainly came to mind. How could they have been so mistaken? Some may have felt misled. Fear led them, like it still does today, to say things regretted later. Perhaps one asked, "Outside of the reference to the temple being rebuilt, do any of you recall any warning that this might have taken place?"

For Peter, this night, like the previous one, was full of guilt and regret. *He'd never forgive me for this even if He were still alive. Why did I boast at the last supper we had together? He said I was a "rock" at one time, but I am not worthy of His trust in me. How did He know I would fail Him?*

Some disciples already had decided to return to their former lines of work. Others planned a Sunday trip to Emmaus. They forgot His instructions of where to meet Him. Was it Galilee or Jerusalem? No matter; if they were going anywhere, it would be in the opposite direction.

It appears as though Jesus' constant lessons to His disciples had been ignored. One disciple was already dead—a traitor. The others seemed to duck for cover now that their Leader was in a tomb guarded by Roman soldiers.

Something powerful and life changing had to occur—and something did!

Peter, the one who denied His Lord, would later write with convincing clarity, "Praise be to the God and Father of our Lord Jesus Christ! In his great mercy he has given us new birth into a living hope *through the resurrection of Jesus Christ from the dead*" (1 Peter 1:3, NIV; emphasis added).

The first to witness the empty tomb were women. In those times, like shepherds, women were not allowed to testify in court because they were deemed unreliable! However, it is Mary who is told to go and tell the disciples "and Peter" (Mark 16:7), who comes to the tomb himself to see if the women's report was correct. He seems mystified. Where had Christ gone? He has gone home!

Something truly powerful takes place on Sunday. On the road to Emmaus and in the closed room with the disciples, Jesus does something that, powered by the Holy Spirit, transforms these disciples. He explains the Scriptures to them—the prophecies and the history. They're all about Him!

Oh to have heard Jesus open the Scriptures and conclude by saying, "Thus it is written, that the Christ would suffer and rise again from the dead the third day" (Luke 24:46, NASB). Jesus was not only alive before them, His mission came alive through the power of understanding God's Word!

Our success is built on the same principle: Study the Word of God. Marinate your mind with it. Let it feed your soul. But always remember the glorious revelation of the Bible. It's all about Jesus!

The disciples would go on to take the gospel from Jerusalem, to Judea and Samaria, and to the ends of the earth as they knew it then. In that day it took less than one generation for the message to reach Rome! It is amazing what can happen when our efforts are combined with the Holy Spirit's power!

Now imagine for a moment that you are at Golgotha. A heavenly painter is recording the scene. Where are you in the picture? Are you going to let Jesus stand alone? I am convinced you won't. You have seen Christ, and you know you want to be by His side. You have studied the Scriptures and are convinced they speak of Jesus and the necessity of being near Him. You wish to be led by the Holy Spirit to proclaim "a risen Savior, He's in the world today!"[3] You are not going to listen to your adversary, the roaring lion. You know you're worthy because Christ died on the cross for you!

So where are you standing? Do you hear His invitation to join Him in the baptism of His death and resurrection to new life? The decision to be baptized is an acceptance of Christ's invitation to die with Him and rise out of the "watery grave" into His resurrection.

Perhaps you can sing along with the song:

I've wasted many precious years, now I'm
coming home;

I now repent with bitter tears; Lord, I'm
coming home.
Coming home, coming home nevermore to
roam;
Open wide Thine arms of love; Lord, I'm
coming home.[4]

The answer to my question of many years ago is now clear. Jesus is not standing alone. Because He did for us what we cannot do for ourselves, we stand with Him, proclaiming to all of the world our belief in His saving grace. Baptism is a public proclamation of our acceptance of that grace.

Visitors to the Hall of the Crucifixion-Resurrection at Glendale's Forest Lawn Cemetery can now see, in addition to Styka's *The Crucifixion,* American painter Robert Clark's painting *The Resurrection.* Completed in 1965, the painting shows Jesus emerging in triumph from the garden tomb and looking forward in faith to the time when the redeemed of the ages will join Him in everlasting glory. It may be something like what John the revelator saw in vision and recorded while he was imprisoned on Patmos:

Then I saw "a new heaven and a new earth,"

> for the first heaven and the first earth had passed away, and there was no longer any sea. I saw the Holy City, the new Jerusalem, coming down out of heaven from God, prepared as a bride beautifully dressed for her husband. And I heard a loud voice from the throne saying, "Look! God's dwelling place is now among the people, and he will dwell with them. They will be his people, and God himself will be with them and be their God. 'He will wipe every tear from their eyes. There will be no more death' or mourning or crying or pain, for the old order of things has passed away" (Revelation 21:1–4, NIV).

I believe that some of the tears that will be wiped away on that day will be the Lord's. For if all of heaven rejoices when a sinner repents, then what does it do when a sinner is lost for eternity?

Is Jesus is crying for you today? If so, if you have any compassion in your heart, take your stand with Jesus today. Say to the world that though Jesus may have died alone, today you are taking your stand with Him for eternity!

Fred Kinsey is the former Director/Speaker of the Voice of Prophecy *radio broadcast.*

---

1. Unless otherwise noted, Bible quotations in this chapter are from the New King James Version of the Bible.

2. "Must Jesus Bear the Cross Alone," in *The Seventh-day Adventist Hymnal* (Hagerstown, Md.: Review and Herald®, 1985), hymn no. 328.

3. "He Lives," in *The Seventh-day Adventist Hymnal* (Hagerstown, Md.: Review and Herald®, 1985), hymn no. 251.

4. "Lord, I'm Coming Home," in *The Seventh-day Adventist Hymnal* (Hagerstown, Md.: Review and Herald®, 1985), hymn no. 296.